Contents

1. Introduction   1
2. Women in Relationship   8
3. The Death Fallacy   35
4. Subverting Stereotypes   52
5. The Short Sharp Shock   69
6. Standing Outside the Mainstream   86
7. The Plath Technique   109
8. Coming Into Her Own   133
9. A Biographical Note   149
Notes   164
Selected Bibliography   204
Index of Poems   215

Permissions

The author would like to thank the following:

Phyllis Chesler, for quotations from *Women and Madness*, published by Avon, 1972.

Another Part of the Fifties, Paul Carter, 1983 © Columbia University Press, New York. Reprinted by permission from the publisher.

Faber and Faber Ltd, for quotations from *The Bed Book*, by Sylvia Plath, 1976; *Collected Poems of Sylvia Plath*, edited by Ted Hughes, 1981; *The Journals of Sylvia Plath*, edited by Ted Hughes and Frances McCullough; and *Letters Home*, edited by Aurelia S Plath, 1975.

Methuen, for quotations from *Man & Work*, by D Meakin, 1976.

Routledge, for quotations from *Man in the Modern Age*, by Karl Jaspers, 1951.

Quotations from *On Lies, Secrets and Silence – Selected Prose 1966–1978*, by Adrienne Rich, are used with the permission of the author and the publisher, W W Norton & Company, Inc. Copyright © 1979 by W W Norton & Company, Inc.; and Virago Press, 1980.

David Riesman, *The Lonely Crowd*, 1950 © Yale University Press, New Haven and London. Reprinted by permission from the publisher.

Every effort has been made to trace the original copyright holders, but in some instances this has not been possible. It is hoped that any such omission from this list will be excused.

Janice Markey has an MA in English, Philosophy and French, an M.Phil. and Ph.D. in English and a BA in Psychology. She has held several teaching appointments in English, French, German and Creative Writing at colleges and universities throughout the UK, Canada and Germany.

She has worked as a stage-manager and PR officer, and as a journalist for a daily newspaper as well as on the Eastern European Desk in the BBC World Service.

A published poet, Janice Markey has written, directed and produced a short film and is currently completing her first novel and screenplay.

First published by The Women's Press Ltd, 1993
A member of the Namara Group
34 Great Sutton Street, London EC1V 0DX

British Library Cataloguing-in-Publication Data
Markey, Janice
Journey into the Red Eye: Poetry of
Sylvia Plath – A Critique
I. Title
811.54

ISBN 0 7043 4316 9

Typeset in 12 on 12pt Times Roman
by The Electronic Book Factory Ltd, Fife, Scotland
Printed and bound in Great Britain by
BPCC Hazells Ltd.
Member of BPCC Ltd.

For Sylvia

> . . . I
> Am the arrow,
>
> The dew that flies
> Suicidal, at one with the drive
> Into the red
>
> Eye, the cauldron of morning.
>
> (Sylvia Plath, 'Ariel')

Acknowledgements

With grateful thanks to my superb editor Loulou Brown and to Kathy Gale; special thanks to Katherine Gallagher, Dorothy McKinley, Harriet Crabtree and Annie Myers and company; to Sarah Black, Barbara Blumenthal and Karen Kukil at the Smith College Rare Book Room, the Neilson Library, Smith College, Northampton, Mass., USA; staff at the BBC Written Archives, Caversham Park, Reading; the National Sound Archive; the British Library; my parents; and Sheila Jeffreys; thanks to Sarah-Jayne, Karen and Neville for their *joie de vivre*; thanks to Karen Chessl, Martin, Michael, Steven and Judith; and thanks to M Gomez for constancy.

1. Introduction

Sylvia Plath is a name now known all over the world. A brilliant and beautiful American writer who committed suicide at the age of 30, her work has been translated into all major languages and has inspired the work of choreographers, rock musicians, composers, playwrights and film-makers, as well as other writers.[1] Yet the achievement of this talented writer remains obscured by an excessive focus on her death as her *raison d'être* and, by extension, the *raison d'être* of her work, as well as of her tempestuous life. Since 1963 at times it has been very clear how biographical criticism, with its obsessive interest in Plath's suicide, can distort the facts. The titles of two of the most recent publications on Plath, Ronald Hayman's biography, *The Death and Life of Sylvia Plath*[2] and Jacqueline Rose's *The Haunting of Sylvia Plath*[3] underscore this.

Biographical criticism is necessarily highly subjective. The biographer's interpretation is coloured by his or her own judgement of the subject's life. Plath has perhaps suffered more than most modern writers from the attentions of critics looking to prove their own psychoanalytic or socio-political beliefs.[4] As a result, much of what has been published on Plath falls into several partisan camps.

The first group comprises those who consider her work to be little more than the expression of a tortured suicidal mind. In one of the earliest published assessments of Plath, *The Savage God: A Study of Suicide*[5] A Alvarez saw her suicide as part of an established tradition, and that it was 'a last desperate attempt to exorcize the death she had summoned up in her poems'.[6] Edward Butscher, the first to publish

1

a 'critical biography' of Plath, regarded Plath's poetry in *Ariel* as having 'deteriorated into a wound'.[7] There was, he suggested, a logical connection between the treatment of death in Plath's poetry and her own death: 'There is nothing left after "Edge" but the finding of the stark suicide note, which is what "Words" is – the last inevitable paragraph in the sequence as a whole.'[8] David Holbrook's *Poetry and Existence*, which drew on 'insights from various forms of psychotherapy'[9] regarded Plath as having a 'false maleness'[10] and a 'topography of her own, which is that of the world as the schizoid individual sees it.'[11] While Butscher and Holbrook held that Plath's work was merely a reflection of her neurosis and self-obsession,[12] they also valued her work as part of a tradition which considered neurosis to be of prime importance.

A commonly held opinion among several critics, including Robert Phillips, Charles Newman (whose selection of essays was the first critical work on Plath[13]) and M L Rosenthal, was that Plath, along with Robert Lowell, Theodore Roethke and Anne Sexton, belonged to the Confessional school of poetry. For the Confessional poets, 'the imaginative realization of dying' was the determining, 'climactic experience of living'[14] while the object of each poem was 'self-therapy and a certain purgation'.[15]

Other critics, including some feminists, regard Plath as a female victim of male oppression. Carole Ferrier, for example, has described her as 'a victim of the fifties and its ideology of the family'.[16] Critics supporting this view, who include Adrienne Rich, argue that the 1950s was an era which was hostile to women, especially to those who were gifted and unconventional.

The bible of that period – Marynia Farnham and Ferdinand Lundberg's *Modern Woman – the lost sex*

(1947) argued that women could only find fulfilment by adopting a passive role, the ultimate goal of which was motherhood.[17] This was very much in keeping with the social and political spirit of the time. With the end of the Second World War, women were urged to give up their work and go back into the home to become full-time mothers and wives, leaving the job market for the male population. This was in part dictated by economic necessity but also by the prevailing conservative ideology. Farnham and Lundberg's book provided justification for women's subordination to men and having their sphere of influence extremely restricted. They suggested that to educate women would lead them away from their 'true' route to satisfaction, as wives and mothers.

As a result of this prevailing climate of opinion, in the USA, the average age of marriage for women decreased from 21.5 years in 1940 to 20.1 in 1956, while the birth rate rose from 19.4 births per 1,000 people in 1940 to 25.3 in 1957. The percentage of women graduates increased by roughly one half during this period, but at the same time the percentage of male graduates vitually doubled.[18]

In her recent psychoanalytical study Jacqueline Rose regards Plath as a fantasy figure,[19] (a stance similar to that adopted by Judith Kroll[20]), and as inconsistent, with no one stable identity.[21] Criticism of Plath has, however, most frequently depicted her as a one-dimensional figure, almost a caricature, shaped by the values and views presented by the particular critic. Such a judgement of Plath, however, is inconsistent with the range of appeal she has for an extensive and eclectic international audience. By relegating her to the position of navel-gazing neurotic, oppressed victim, self-mythologiser or academic, critics have failed to account for the reasons for Plath's fame and appeal. And by assessing the writer solely according to their views on how she lived her life, they have failed to do justice to her work.

Her work may confound and shock, but it never fails to leave an impact. Roland Barthes' call for the death of the author – 'Writing is that neuter, that composite, that obliquity into which our subject flees, the black-and-white where all identity is lost, beginning with the very identity of the body that writes'[22] – is especially relevant in the case of Plath, whose last published poem 'Words'[23] is in praise of the independence of the work from the writer. Plath was above all else a writer, and she believed in the power of her work.

This book is concerned with the poetry of Sylvia Plath. Where biographical facts can help to expand and illuminate, they will be included, but my focus is on Plath's poetry, its style and content. I argue that Plath's voice is consistent, and that her moral and philosophical stance is equally consistent throughout all her work.

Plath's poetry has a universal appeal, which extends beyond national and social barriers, her work attracting the interest of a wide public. While it deals in part with 'women's issues', many critics and writers, such as Seamus Heaney, Eric Homberger, A Alvarez, Ronald Hayman, Alan Brownjohn, Peter Porter and Michael Horowitz, have testified to its appeal to men as well as women.[24] The voice was original and distinctive and, I believe, it will continue to be relevant and important, by virtue of its wide range of social and moral concerns and the appeal and impact of the Plath technique.

With her treatment of the theme of personal relationships (see Chapter 2), Plath subverted a subject considered in the 1950s by the male writing establishment to be appropriate for women writers. The dearth of poems on successful relations between

4

the sexes directly stems from the overwhelming sense of aridity and destructiveness which Plath, like D H Lawrence and Virginia Woolf before her, saw to be the result of patriarchal culture. Her deflation of prescribed femininity and exposure of sado-masochism in gender-defined roles led her to disavow the ideal of romantic love as a myth, which trivalises women's feelings and makes them powerless. Her strong empathy with women became increasingly more evident at the end of her life, with the sympathetic views towards relationships between women in her work. And Plath's eloquent love poems to her children present a new and realistic assessment of both the depths and limitations of the mother-child relationship, again defying conventional mores and representations.

Much of the controversy and misinterpretation of Plath's work is owing to an excessive emphasis on her periods of depression and her suicide. Critics who accuse Plath of regarding death as a means of rebirth and purification are not supported by the textual evidence. Plath's tongue-in-cheek deflation of the Female Gothic and her evident hatred of death in any form are the motivating forces behind her handling of this theme as evidenced in Chapter 3. More than has ever before been acknowledged, her death was an ill-timed cry for help.

Plath's preoccupation with religious themes stems from the tradition of High Idealism and was further motivated by her empathy with Unitarianism. Chapter 4 shows how she regarded conventional religion as an extension of patriarchal ideology, and her confrontation with this ideology and exposé of its figureheads and ministers and subservient female images reinforced her belief that existentialism was the only honest belief system. Attracted to mysticism, Plath remained curious about the afterlife, but was nevertheless firmly rooted in an appreciation of life in the here and now.

Because of the excessive interest in her suicide, the humour in Plath's poetry has been largely overlooked. This has resulted in a distortion of the overall effect of her work. Plath's writing abounds in one-liners, subversive, impertinent jibes at the status quo and mock-Gothic scenarios. A look at her use of humour in Chapter 5 reveals just how expansive and imaginative her perspective was. Humour was an important tool in her protest against the conservative attitudes, beliefs and values which prevailed in the 1950s with the rigid prescribed roles for both men and women.

Plath was a writer who was well-read and deeply concerned about the issues of her time. She was very aware of the dangers of a misuse of technology, the logical result of which was the exploitation of humanity – seen at its most depraved in the mechanical dehumanised world of the death camps – and of the environment. Her poems expose the risks of consumerism, the immense, insidious power of the advertising industry in the 1950s, with the ominous, anonymous threat of faceless bureaucracy ready to introduce war for profit. Her poems on these themes, as demonstrated in Chapter 6, show the strong, humanist concern she had for the preservation of all life and her concern for the environment.

At the beginning of her writing career, Plath used a variety of symbols and techniques, derived from Greek and other mythologies, to provide a supporting contextual framework for her poetry. When she found her own voice, however, she discarded these and instead created her own elaborate, interwoven world of symbols and images and cinematic techniques which helped to mark out her unique form of expression. Her use of language is striking as shown

6

in Chapter 7, often shocking and multilayered, and her use of symbols can be construed as feminist in its reversal of gender-defined meaning.

At first influenced by the great modern writers, she became increasingly more drawn to the work of women writers, and indeed regarded herself as part of their great tradition, extending back through the centuries with a special affinity to those from North America. Towards the end of her life she ceased to make the compromise she had previously lived with and accepted her identity as a rebel against a stultifying and oppressive tradition, while she regarded herself as a spokesperson for the disenfranchised and the voiceless, a role she thought a writer should adopt.

A study of Plath's themes as set out in Chapter 8 shows that hers was no narrow, self-obsessed vision, but one that clearly marked her as a major writer. Her themes were universal.[25] Hers was an original voice, immensely powerful, and she fused her content with a language that expressed a vision of compassion and sanity.

2. Women in Relationship

Much criticism of Plath and her work has focused on the notion that her vision was egocentric. As a result, the many poems she wrote on the theme of personal relationships have not been accorded sufficient interest. An analysis of Plath's poems on this theme, however, reveals that relationships were in fact extremely important to her.

Plath focused on men's deficiencies and how they made heterosexual relationships problematic. Her poems, specifically related to the sado-masochism underlying such relationships, show that she saw romantic love as a shallow myth which trivialised women's lives and rendered them powerless. It is also clear that she regarded the patriarchal structure of society to be inimical for both sexes. In addition she wrote poems about women in relationships with each other and these tended to depict such relationships in a very negative light. It is significant, however, that the one poem on relationships which centres on fulfilment and ends on a positive note ('Ariel,' *CP* 239–40) focuses on a relationship between two women. Plath also writes in a radical and innovative way about the mother-daughter relationship and on motherhood. The poems are very far from conventional representations on the subject and explore the inherent dual tensions.

Some of her poems, of course, were merely based on real events. But any poet's work is also an act of creative imagination and literary criticism can draw conclusions from that creation about the poet's perspective.

Plath dealt with personal relationships in a way that openly challenged the prevailing social mores.

8

Her poems show that, far from being hostile to, and suspicious of, other women, as many critics have claimed, she was very much a woman-centred poet.

Towards the end of her life, particularly during the last six months, Plath was writing poems which challenged the status quo. There was nothing genteel or anything at all conventional about these writings which have ever since provided a platform for feminist and other women writers. Her contemporary Adrienne Rich has characterised Plath's work as follows:

> . . . it is finally the woman's sense of herself – embattled, possessed – that gives the poetry its dynamic charge, its rhythms of struggle, need, will, and female energy. Until recently this female anger and this furious awareness of the Man's power over her were not available materials to the female poet, who tended to write of Love as the source of her suffering, and to view that victimization by Love as an almost inevitable fate. Or, like Marianne Moore and Elizabeth Bishop, she kept sexuality at a measured and chiseled distance in her poems.[1]

Although Marianne Moore and Elizabeth Bishop were, as several of Plath's journal entries and letters indicate, initial role models for her work[2] she soon left them far behind in her treatment of personal relations.

From the days of her childhood, Plath had idolised all the men in her life. Such idolatory which was reflected in her poetry (for example in 'Daddy') was later to cause her much angst when the men she idolised failed to live up to her very high expectations. Plath also had very strong erotic tendencies,[3] and there is evidence in her poetry of an erotic attraction

9

to women, which has almost completely been ignored. Initially, Plath only partly accepted these tendencies, because she at first wanted to conform to the 1950s' female role-model.

> I am part man, and I notice women's breasts and thighs with the calculation of a man choosing a mistress . . . but that is the artist and the analytical attitude towards the female body . . . for I am more a woman; even as I long for full breasts and a beautiful body, so do I abhor the sensuousness which they bring.[4]

There is, however, a chronological development in Plath's poetry about relationships, which shows that while heterosexual relationships appear increasingly doomed to failure, the possibility of successful relationships between women is ultimately left open.

Men's deficiencies

Plath's treatment of relationships between men and women explodes the 1950s' myth of happy domesticity.[5] Such relationships are demystified and a realistic and ultimately pessimistic view of their success is presented. Poems celebrating successful heterosexual relationships are singularly few; when they do occur it is within the realm of fantasy, as illustrated by the poems 'Ode for Ted' (*CP*, pp. 29–30), a romantic eulogy, and 'Two Views of a Cadaver Room' (*CP*, p. 114) based on a painting by Breughel, which depicts an imagined relationship: '. . . desolation, stalled in paint, spares the little country/Foolish, delicate, in the lower right hand corner.'[6]

Most of Plath's poems on relationships focus on the failure of heterosexual relations, while the opening

10

and close of Plath's version of *Ariel*, as indicated by Ted Hughes in a note at the end of *The Collected Poems*,[7] clearly shows where she placed the emphasis in personal relations towards the end of her life. It begins with a poem to her daughter, the first word being 'love' ('Morning Song'), and ends with the word 'spring' ('Wintering'), which concluded a poem envisaging a world of female bees without drones. As Plath in a cycle of poems on the world of bees – 'The Bee Meeting' (*CP*, pp. 211–12), 'The Arrival of the Bee Box' (*CP*, pp. 212–13), 'Stings' (*CP*, pp. 214–15), 'The Swarm' (*CP*, pp. 215–17) – identified the female speaker in the poems with the role of queen bee, the ending of this poem implies a woman imagining life in a world without men.[8]

Relations between men and women often founder because of what Plath regarded as men's inherent deficiencies. Several poems criticise men for being flat, sterile and unimaginative.[9] They are responsible for 'That flat, flat, flatness from which ideas, destructions/Bulldozers, guillotines, white chambers of shrieks proceed . . .' ('Three Women', *CP*, pp. 176–87.)

As 'Gigolo' (*CP*, pp. 267–8) indicates, men are also egocentric; the poem is a witty pastiche on the male ego and male sexual prowess. In this bawdily-worded piece, the gigolo is set up as a caricature of manhood, a self-obsessed narcissist who delights in his collection of smiling women who 'Gulp at my bulk' while deifying himself sexually: 'My mouth sags,/The mouth of Christ/When my engine reaches the end of it.' The end of every action, including sex, is himself: 'All the fall of water an eye/Over whose pool I tenderly/lean and see me.' Other negative attributes Plath ascribed to men surface here, too – their need to use and exploit, whether in relations with others or with the environment.

An even more disconcerting character defect is the inherent trend in men towards wanton violence and destructiveness. This is the theme of several poems.[10] It runs through 'Pheasant' (*CP*, p. 191) where the female narrator is forced to beg her male companion for the life of the pheasant which has suddenly appeared on the property. It is the theme of 'Zoo Keeper's Wife' (*CP*, pp. 154–5) in which the wife lives out a nightmarish existence in a claustrophobic and abusive relationship with her husband: '. . . Tangled in the sweat-wet sheets/I remember the bloodied chicks and the quartered rabbits.'

Similarly, the rabbit catcher in the poem of the same name (*CP*, pp. 193–4) thrives on the savage and bloody deaths of his prey:

How they awaited him those little deaths!
They awaited like sweethearts.
They excited him.

Inimical and sadistic to the environment around them, men in Plath's poetry, particularly in her later work, also appear sadistic in their relations with women. In 'The Rabbit Catcher' the relationship the man has with his female companion is compared to his relationship with the prey he kills; he has:

. . . a mind like a ring
Sliding shut on some quick thing,
The constriction killing me also.[11]

Plath's poetry throughout seems marked by an extreme distrust of man's ability to form relationships, as the slyly cynical poem 'Strumpet Song' (*CP*, pp. 33–4), written early in her career, indicated. A sorry figure, the strumpet, a term loaded with considerable irony, awaits a perverse Prince Charming 'To patch with brand of love this rank grimace'. The love men have for women is regarded as a 'brand'; violence is omnipresent. Similarly, the spinster ('Spinster', *CP*, pp. 49–50) finds no difficulty in resisting the amorous advances of her male companion, since beneath them she perceives a latent violence masquerading as love. She creates barriers such as: . . . no mere insurgent man could hope to break/With curse, fist, threat/Or love, either.

Sado-masochistic relations

In Plath's later poems, women are regarded as the angels in the house, naturally submissive to their husbands and mentors.[12] But they reverse the process in a startling and powerful manner. 'Purdah' (*CP*, pp. 242–3), for instance, focuses on the plight of the female slave in the harem, the eastern equivalent of the 'living doll', who, as the scope of the poem enlarges, becomes every woman. She is scarcely more than a possession of her master, unable to live out her own life:

Even in his

absence, I
Revolve in my
Sheath of impossibles . . .

At the end of the poem, however, the victim takes her revenge and assumes the identity of every abused woman in history. She becomes an awesome composite of Charlotte Corday and Medea:

. . . at his next step
I shall unloose

I shall unloose –

13

From the small jewelled
Doll he guards like a heart —

The lioness,
The shriek in the bath,
The cloak of holes.[13]

The sado-masochism underlying heterosexual relations is most horrifically depicted in a later poem
'The Jailer' (CP, pp. 226–7), in which each facet of
the relationship subjects the woman to torture and
continual rape, while liberation from this situation is
seen to be impossible:

. . . What would the dark
Do without fevers to eat?
What would the light
Do without eyes to knife, what would he
Do, do, do without me?

It would be both simplistic and unreasonable to indict
men only for the difficulty in establishing and maintaining positive heterosexual relations, and Plath consciously avoids this trap. Rather, she locates part of
the reason for such poor relationships in the psyche
of women and in socialisation processes.[14] Thus, in
'Widow' (CP, pp. 164–5), the woman lives a shadowy
existence, unable to free herself from the influence of
her dead husband: 'Death is the dress she wears, her
hat and collar'. She is depicted as a 'bitter spider',
sitting 'in the center of her loveless spokes'. She
unnecessarily intensifies her suffering and opts for a
situation she recognises is self-destructive. The biblical concept of woman as part of man, which reinforces
the subordination of women, assumes a horrific significance in 'Getting There' (CP, pp. 247–49); '. . . It
is Adam's side,/This earth I rise from, and I in agony',
the female speaker declares.

Common to 'Daddy' and to a number of poems was the idea of sex between men and being torture for women. Plath's poems on t daughter relationship follow along similar lines. Subject to a forbidden eroticism[15] this relationship is also very much one dominated by sado-masochistic tendencies. 'Daddy' (*CP*, pp. 222–4) was a vehicle for Plath's assessment of the relationship between father and daughter, and by extension the nature of relations between men and women. In a commentary for a broadcast of the poem she described the poem as follows:

> The poem is spoken by a girl with an Electra complex. Her father died while she thought he was God. Her case is complicated by the fact that her father was also a Nazi and her mother very possibly part-Jewish. In the daughter the two strains marry and paralyse each other – she has to act out the awful little allegory before she is free of it.[16]

In 'Daddy' the idolised male/father/husband is 'A man in black with a Meinkampf look/And a love of the rack and the screw',[17] and the root of the horror is the reader's realisation that this notion of the father/daughter relationship has so wormed its way into the psyche of women that they have come to believe it is instinctive to adore: '. . . a Fascist,/The boot in the face, the brute/Brute heart of a brute like you.'

In this poem the daunting father figure of 'Colossus' becomes reduced to human size and is stripped of all the destructiveness and abusive power he previously wielded. Having previously been a caricature of evil – 'Not God but a swastika' – a frightening figure the female speaker has lived in terror of, the father now becomes merely a teacher standing at the blackboard, someone vulnerable, whose impending amputation is alluded to – 'A cleft in your chin instead of your foot'. The poem ends with the ultimate reduction of his power as he lies in his grave reviled by the villagers. Plath makes it clear in this poem that the exploitation of women in a patriarchal society is in part due to women's compliance in the sado-masochism involved. The poem moves towards a deconstruction of the myth of the father's right to dominate, a 'vampire' draining the woman's energy. The only way to renounce the negative power of the father is through open rebellion and the poem closes with an act of absolute insubordination. The poem is a supreme example of defiance and an act suggesting liberation from heterosexual opposition. In tone it is similar to the language of violence and revenge in the poetry of Plath's contemporary Adrienne Rich and radical feminist poets of the 1960s and 1970s, such as Robin Morgan, Audre Lorde and Judy Grahn, who called on women to 'reject tokenism, turn their backs on patriarchy and attempts to reform it, and to embark on the journey to the Otherworld'[18]:

> There's a stake in your fat black heart
> And the villagers never liked you.
> They are dancing and stamping on you.
> They always *knew* it was you.
> Daddy, daddy, you bastard, I'm through.

The nightmare of sado-masochistic relations between men and women unfolds most menacingly in Plath's 'concentration camp' poems, especially in 'Lady Lazarus' (*CP*, pp. 244–7), where the woman, reduced to an object:

> . . . my skin
> Bright as a Nazi lampshade,

My right foot
A paperweight,
My face a featureless, fine
Jew linen.

becomes an avenging phoenix ready to extract her
own vengeance on her male abusers, Herr Doctor,
Herr Lucifer:

Out of the ash
I rise with my red hair
And I eat men like air.

Another poem 'Fever 103°' (*CP*, pp. 231–2) also refutes
the possibility of positive heterosexual relations.[19] After
three days and nights of sex[20] the woman seeks release
from her male lover, placing herself literally above
him, in an ironic role reversal. The assumption of
godliness is in this poem used as a means of release
from a shabby existence, which, as Plath intimates
here, is the real meaning of purification. The woman in
'Fever 103°' purges herself of all earthly encumbrances,
including her male lover, a relationship she associates
with prostitution: '(My selves, dissolving, old whore
petticoats)-/To Paradise.'[21]

Plath's analysis of heterosexual relations ended with
her realisation that the great ideal of romantic love
between men and women was nothing more than a
myth which trivialised women's feelings and rendered
them powerless. Patriarchal society contributes to
this, by prioritising male dominance and encouraging
a victim mentality in women. In the poem 'Mystic'
(*CP*, pp. 268–9), written just before she died, Plath
wrote 'Is there no great love, only tenderness?' This
insight, it is suggested, did not mean that she dismissed
the possibility of successful personal relations; rather,

it signalled in fact that her concern for such relations led her in another direction, one that was unconventional for her time – to consider relationships between women.

Women in relationship

Plath wrote a number of poems about relationships between women. Her *Journals* show that tenderness was a quality she readily associated with lesbian relationships.[22] In *The Bell Jar*, Doctor Nolan, the psychiatrist, who is the one female character depicted in a positive way in the book, and the only one the heroine, Esther, will listen to, gives the following response:

> 'I don't see what women see in other women'; I'd told Doctor Nolan in my interview that noon. 'What does a woman see in a woman that she can't see in a man?'
>
> Doctor Nolan paused. Then she said, 'Tenderness'.
>
> That shut me up.[23]

Plath regarded her friendship with room-mates at Smith, Marcia Plumer and Nancy Hunter Steiner, as very important.[24] She wrote of her ambition of becoming 'a woman famous among women'[25] and in 1959 she commented on the change of direction in her work: 'How odd, men don't interest me at all now, only women and women-talk.'[26] She spoke of dedicating a book to her two role-models cum heroines Dr Beuscher, her therapist and Professor Krook, her lecturer on Lawrence and the moralists at Cambridge: 'I, in my sphere, taking my place beside Dr Beuscher and Doris Krook in theirs – neither psychologist, priestess nor philosopher-teacher but a blending of both rich vocations in my own worded world.'27

There are passages in the *Journals* which would appear to point toward erotic experiences with women,28 although since the *Journals* have been subject to stringent censorship, the extent of these relations remains largely undefined. What is certain is that Plath's last poems on relationships centred on those between women: erotic, sexual and emotional. Significantly, her layout of *Ariel* ended with the poem 'Wintering' (*CP*, p. 214). In this poem, the last of the bee cycle poems, only the females survive, having '. . . got rid of the men/The blunt, clumsy stumblers, the boors.' At the end of the poem the females are in ascendancy, 'flying', sampling 'the Christmas roses'29 and tasting 'the spring'.30

The poems she wrote on erotic relationships between women place her in a long established tradition going back through Virginia Woolf, Christina Rossetti and Emily Dickinson.31 Arguably her earliest poem on the theme is 'Leaving Early' (*CP*, pp. 145–6), written in 1960 about an unsatisfying sexual experience with a woman. Critical opinion differs as to whether Plath intended the narrator to be male. Assumptions to that effect have been rejected by feminists as indicative of a wish to suppress evidence of erotic relationships between women.32 But the Plath Estate has pointed to a factual basis for this belief.33 Plath apparently derived the idea for the poem from a male/female relationship known to her and based it on a man's monologue as he left a women. However, the fact that Plath was herself a woman, writing about a sexual relationship with a woman is in itself significant at this stage of her poetic development, and, fascinatingly, the sex of the persona, while its starting point was apparently, in reality, conceived from a male viewpoint, appears to be deliberately ambiguous. For example the speaker

19

addresses the geraniums as 'friends'. They hold positive memories: '. . . They stink of armpits/And the
involved maladies of autumn,/Musky as a lovebed
the morning after.' The reference to 'stink of armpits'
suggests men and the lovebed remembered is 'musky'
in comparison to the one the speaker finds herself in
the poem. 'Musky' is more readily associated with
male scent, which would indicate that the experience
remembered here is with a man. This leaves two interpretations: either the speaker is a man, remembering
a homosexual experience – unlikely since there is no
dramatic reason for this[34] – or the speaker is female,
remembering a far more satisfactory experience with
a man. This interpretation is supported by the fact
that the majority of Plath's poems, especially those
written at this time, have a female speaker, and one
who seems to embody the authorial approach; by the
secrecy surrounding the identity of the speaker; and
by the poem's all-pervasive indirectness. Immediately
after what would appear to have been the love scene,
conspicuously not mentioned, come the lines:

> The roses in the toby jug
> Gave up the ghost last night. High time.
> Their yellow corsets were ready to split.

The flowers act as a metaphor for the speaker/pro-
tagonist, thus distancing the narrator, and the poem
continues in the same vein. The tone of the poem
is one of regret and bitterness, perhaps beyond
the level which could be expected of a socially
acceptable heterosexual relationship. Assuming the
poem does touch on relationships between women,
it is interesting to examine this tone. 'This mizzle fits
me like a sad jacket', the speaker observes, the rain
a metaphor for tears. The night and the experience
have been frustrating and disappointing. Like the

flowers in their various states of disarray and decay, the speaker has been ignored and neglected while the woman in the bed dozes 'nose to the wall'. 'How did we make it up to your attic?' the narrator asks.[35] Drinking 'gin in a glass bud vase' the couple ended up falling asleep: 'We slept like stones.'[36] Like the roses, the speaker too 'gave up the ghost':

I heard the petals unlatch,
Tapping and ticking like nervous fingers.
You should have junked them before they died

The death of expectation is the significance of what has happened here. The poem ends with the speaker lying 'With a lung full of dust and a tongue of wood, /Knee-deep in the cold and swamped by flowers', a state alarmingly similar to being in a grave. The poem has come full circle from the first line, 'your room is lousy with flowers', but instead of, as the title suggests, 'Leaving Early', and she declares this as her expectation in the second line – 'When you kick me out' – the speaker has become paralysed and left in a state without volition of her own. Like other Plath poems written around this period, this poem is woman-centred. What is being condemned in this poem is not the notion of intimacy between women, but the self-centredness of the other woman who has left the speaker lying frozen, emotionally and physically. The attic, with its velvet pillows, is furnished in a style reminiscent of the gigolo's 'palace of velvet', a narcissistic environment.[37]

Two years later Plath wrote a much more direct poem about the possibility of a relationship between women. In 'Lesbos' (*CP*, pp. 227–9)[38] Plath has moved from the discreet externalised hints between women to a direct proposition from one to another. Here the speaker immediately considers the idea of an affair:

I should sit on a rock off Cornwall and comb
   my hair.
I should wear tiger pants,[39] I should have an
   affair.
We should meet in another life, we should meet in
   air,
Me and you.

These words are reminiscent of 'Leaving Early' where
the speaker was described as 'bored as a leopard'
and the currents of bitterness and resentment pervading this poem, underlined by the repetition of the
consonant 's', echo the earlier work, suggesting that
Plath was thinking about the same subject in both.
Here again these currents make it clear that no easy
happy ending for the two protagonists is envisaged.
Their relations have no secure foundation in reality:
the setting is '. . . all Hollywood, windowless', in
what Plath with great irony describes as the natural
domain for women – there is 'Viciousness in the
kitchen'. This is clearly no idyllic Lesbos just as the
experience in 'Leaving Early' was far from ideal. In
fact, everything right from the beginning conspires
against any meaningful relationship between the two
women. There seems to be an incompatibility – the
women are depicted as 'two venomous opposites' even
as they start to make love. And there is no doubt
about the sexual preference of the other woman. The
women are joined by the other woman's husband and
a *ménage à trois* ensues which soon becomes nothing
more than a sordid ritual, because of what the speaker
regards as the bestial nature of the husband: 'A dog
picked up your doggy husband. He went on.' The
intense regret felt by the speaker at the failure of the
relationship is very apparent – she describes herself
as '. . . silent, hate/Up to my neck'. She addresses
her opposite number, disappointed at her inability to

see her predicament and make the right choices: 'O vase of acid,/It is love you are full of. You know who you hate.'[40] She tries to impress on her friend how she is letting herself be used: 'Every day you fill him with soul-stuff, like a pitcher.' But in spite of her attempts to break through, no genuine contact is established. On her way out of her friend's home, the speaker comments on her sensuousness: 'I see your cute décor/Close on you like the fist of a baby' and still allows some physical intimacy: 'Your voice my ear-ring,/Flapping and sucking, blood-loving bat', even while she registers displeasure at her friend's disloyalty towards her sex and towards her: '. . . Every woman's a whore./I can't communicate'. The experience the speaker has made in this poem is incomplete, spoiled – 'I am still raw' she concludes[41] and in bitterness and regret denies the likelihood of taking up this relationship again:

I say I may be back.
You know what lies are for.

Even in your Zen heaven we shan't meet.

The idea here is not that women are emotionally incompatible, as was intimated in 'Leaving Early', but that the relationship is doomed from the start by external forces. It is envisaged as taking place 'in air', while the actual setting is the claustrophobic kitchen with 'The smog of cooking, the smog of hell' which envelops the women in the realm of nightmare. Although she knows her husband is draining her, the wife is unable to leave. She is equally unable to end her affair with her female lover; trapped as she is, a victim ('The sun gives you ulcers, the wind gives you T.B.'). The last statement in the poem, 'Even in your Zen heaven we shan't meet', far from being an indictment of relations between women, is actually a regret at the way socialisation has isolated women and taught them to regard each other as natural enemies and rivals.[42] The woman lives in a state of angry frustration at her own paralysis, a frustration seething even during sex: '. . . the lightning./The acid baths, the skyfuls off of you.'

'Eavesdropper' (*CP*, pp. 260–1) is a chilling description of one woman by another, chilling because of the other woman's personality. She is described in singularly unflattering terms: 'Mole on my shoulder', 'The stain of the tropics/Still urinous on you', 'You may be local,/But that yellow!/Godawful!' The Plath Estate has pointed out that this poem was based on an actual situation, a resented intrusion in Plath's life and that it therefore cannot be considered as a reflection by Plath on affairs between women. I would argue that the dramatic movement metamorphoses the initial real-life situation and that the poem assumes overtones of an erotic and sado-masochistic nature, centred around the imbalance of power in the relations between the two women. There is a taint of perversity and immorality about the woman described here:

> Tarting with the drafts that pass,
> Little whore tongue,
> Chenille beckoner,

These lines are clearly erotic and carry sado-masochistic overtones. The speaker does not gain from this relationship:

> Your body one
> Long nicotine-finger

On which I,
White cigarette,
Burn, for your inhalation,
Driving the dull cells wild.

Let me roost in you!

The last line here is a clear expression of desire. In the original manuscript of the poems, at Smith College, the following lines, which indicate that the lover is female, are omitted after the third draft:

I have seen your face
Lady, lady, pale as steam
Flatten or vanish
in window after window

Here, what at first sight seems to have taken on a new meaning to signify phallic imagery – 'finger' and 'cigarette' – have taken on a new meaning to signify female power and activity, while the last line – 'Let me roost in you!' – shows without doubt that sexual dominance lies with the speaker. Throughout this poem the speaker seems to have resigned herself to a bleak future:

This is what I am in for –
Flea body!
Eyes like mice

The last line of the poem underscores the paralysing ambivalence of the speaker's feelings about the relationship: 'Toad-stone! Sister-bitch! Sweet neighbor.' 'Toad-stone' indicates the sexual dominance of the speaker and carries the suggestion of sado-masochistic relations.

In 'Elm' (an earlier poem written in April 1962, *CP*,

25

pp. 192–3) the aftermath of sex once more results in frustration and deep despair. Again, horseriding is the accompaniment to the erotic subtext:

All night I shall gallop thus, impetuously,
Till your head is a stone, your pillow a little turf,
Echoing, echoing.

But here, in comparison to the positive exuberance of 'Ariel' where the movement is into dawn, the speaker has 'suffered the atrocity of *sunsets*'.[43] Her lover is described as 'merciless' and plaguing her with nightmares: 'How your bad dreams possess and endow me.' The end of this relationship is horrific. The lover, destructive in her self-obsessiveness, is a Medusa-like figure, '. . . this face/So murderous in its strange of branches' while 'Its snaky acids kiss.' At the end of this poem the speaker is once more left in a paralysing ambivalence, which, it is suggested, will turn out to be fatal:[44]

It petrifies the will. These are the isolate, slow faults
That kill, that kill, that kill.

In the manuscript of this poem at Smith in draft 3a, the following lines appear, emphasising the sex of the speaker's counterpart: 'Do I need such a false relation?/She upsets me some way.'

'Winter Trees' (*CP*, pp. 257–8), written in November 1962, expresses regret for the failure of relationships between women. As the speaker looks around her, she compares the constancy of the trees to inconstancy in personal relations. They seem to her:

Memories growing, ring on ring.
A series of weddings,

26

> Knowing neither abortions nor bitchery,
> Truer than women.

Significantly, in Plath's work there is virtually no poem on friendship which is not explicitly sexual. 'The Babysitters' (*CP* pp. 174–5) seems at first sight to be an exception. In this poem the speaker regrets the passing of friendship and the separation which appears to have been enforced by external factors:

> The shadows of the grasses inched round like hands
>   of a clock,
> And from our opposite continents we wave and call.
> Everything has happened.

The passing of innocence – there are numerous references to 'Alice in Wonderland' – has also entailed the end of an uncomplicated friendship. Yet even this relationship is not equivocal; the friendship is an intimate one: the speaker describes herself and her friend as 'inseparable', while the change in their circumstances seems to threaten her happiness: 'What keyhole have we slipped through, what door has shut?'

In an interesting contrast, Plath's poems on heterosexual relations (with the exception of 'Zoo Keeper's Wife' and 'The Rival', which deal with the woman's subordination to her male partner), focus on absence and distance, while her poems on relationships between women focus on the intense and, at times, claustrophobic intimacy of the relationships.

Fulfilment

The negative poems on the theme of relationships between women, and especially those written towards the end of Plath's life, show not that Plath discarded the viability of this form of relationship but rather that she found the outcome disappointing, with the potential of such relationships thwarted by external forces. It is important to note that her views on this theme seem to have been coloured by the nature of the women she depicts in these poems. They are either trapped in socially constricting roles or are selfish and extremely narcissistic. The one exception is 'Ariel', and it is significant that this is a poem which, instead of locking into one narrow segment of life – like, for instance, the smog-filled enclosure of the kitchen hell in 'Lesbos', the claustrophobic attic room of 'Leaving Early' and the nightmarish bedrooms of 'Eavesdropper' and 'Elm' – opens up the speaker's world into three levels, as she finds a spiritual and physical redemption through sex, an active involvement in the world around her and creativity in art.

'Ariel' deals with a sexual encounter between two women, but this time ends on a note of power and affirmation. Written on Plath's birthday, a day she considered particularly auspicious, 'Ariel' is highly erotic. It is also complex and dynamic. Its title is drawn from the spirit Ariel in Shakespeare's *The Tempest*, one of her favourite plays. It refers, in a biblical sense, to Jerusalem as the scene of a holocaust which burned sacrificial victims,[45] and also to the horse Plath was learning to ride. The action of the poem takes place on three levels: a sexual experience, horseriding[46] and the creation of a work of art. On the sexual level it becomes obvious from the imagery that it is an experience with a woman which is being described. The first indication of this is the speaker – and here there is no disputing the fact that the speaker is female – addressing her lover as 'God's lioness'. The interaction between the women makes this apparent:

Pivot of heels and knees! – The furrow

Splits and passes, *sister*[47] to
The brown arc
Of the neck I cannot catch

In the third draft of this poem, which resides at Smith, Plath had the unequivocal line: 'Pivot of heels and knees, and of my color.'

In 'Ariel', replete with female symbols only ('furrow' – vagina, 'neck' – cervix, 'black sweet blood mouthfuls' – menstrual blood, 'wall' – the wall of the vagina, 'the red/Eye' – vagina), the speaker moves from complete passivity, the 'Stasis in darkness', to active involvement:

Something else

Hauls me through air –
Thighs, hair;
Flakes from my heels.

The movement is positive – she becomes free of all the draining encumbrances of her previous life.

. . . I unpeel –
Dead hands, dead stringencies.

The sex involved here entails no risk of pregnancy so 'The child's cry/Melts in the wall', while the moment of orgasm is one of great intimacy with the lover: '. . . now I/Foam to wheat, a glitter of seas.'[48] The effect of the sexual interaction here is unequivocally positive: it emancipates the speaker, who then turns wholeheartedly to the quest for autonomy and creativity:

. . . I
Am the arrow,

29

The dew that flies
Suicidal, at one with the drive
Into the red

Eye, the cauldron of morning.

The poem moves from darkness to morning, from isolation to integration and intimacy, suicidal only in the sense that there is an escape from the claustrophobically isolated personal sphere into a feeling of being at one with the world, the 'red/Eye', simultaneously the womb, the sunrise and the realm of art and creativity – 'the cauldron of morning'.[49]

The mother-daughter relationship

In her two explicit poems on the mother-daughter relationship, 'Medusa' (*CP*, pp. 224–6) and 'The Disquieting Muses' (*CP*, pp. 74–6), Plath showed how identity can be suffocated and the daughter made into a victim.

'Medusa' shows the ambivalent, claustrophobic dependency inherent in the relationship. The unattractiveness of the title indicates the threatening nature of the mother-daughter relationship which is shown to be stifling and an acute interference in the daughter's attempts to live her own life:

. . . you are always there,
Tremulous breath at the end of my line,
Curve of water upleaping
To my water rod, dazzling and grateful,
Touching and sucking.

The automatic reaction is rejection: 'I shall take no bite of your body,/Bottle in which I live,' is the daughter's defiant statement, yet the second line indicates that enforced intimacy is unavoidable. This idea is emphasised by the last ambivalent line of the poem: 'There is nothing between us.' (In 'The Disquieting Muses', an earlier poem, the mother's power is shown to be tenuous, and her judgement flawed.) The mother-daughter relationship is criticised for the mother's oppressive dependency and the daughter's unquestioning obedience, while at the same time the strength of the intimacy is acknowledged.

Concern for children

Plath's poems on children are remarkable for their lyrical beauty and gentle humour and are written from the point of view of a woman bringing up children on her own.

As a mother herself, Plath was not only very concerned about the future and welfare of her own two children but also that of children worldwide. But her poems on the subject also reflect an ambivalence in the relationship between mother and children. In the opinion of M D Uroff, Plath wrote more poems on motherhood than on any other subject. 'It is a point worth noting not only because it must serve to revise her reputation as a death-ridden poet but because a concentration on maternal themes is almost unique among serious poets.'[50]

Plath also has an ambivalent attitude towards pregnancy, reflected in her verse play 'Three Women' which revolves around the very different experiences of three women about to give birth. For the woman behind the First Voice the experience of waiting to give birth makes her feel, 'I am a great event'. The woman behind the Second Voice, however, who has a miscarriage, is 'a garden of black and red agonies', while the Third Voice, with an unwanted pregnancy, declares herself 'not ready for anything to

31

happen./I should have murdered this, that murders me.' The poem 'Metaphors' (*CP*, p. 116), which starts off with some playfully humorous descriptions of pregnancy, ends with the ambiguous two lines which have an element of fatality: 'I've eaten a bag of green apples,/Boarded the train there's no getting off.'

It is fitting that Plath chose a poem to her daughter to be the opening poem of the *Ariel* collection. Starting on the word 'Love', 'Morning Song' (*CP*, pp. 156–7) traces the birth of the relationship between the mother and new-born child. Plath claims there are no ready-made connections: relationships have to be created. As she commented in her *Journals*: 'children might humanize me. But I must rely on them for nothing. Fable of children changing existence and character as absurd as fable of marriage doing it.'[51]

The birth of the child at first endangers the mother's existence in this poem: '. . . your nakedness/shadows our safety', and it seems almost an alien being with its 'moth-breath' that 'Flickers among the flat pink roses' and its mouth that 'opens clean as a cat's'. The child intrudes on what seems an orderly lifestyle – its 'bald cry' taking 'its place among the elements'. Yet, by virtue of its presence it introduces a new beauty into the mother's jaded life:

. . . you try
Your handful of notes;
The clear vowels rise like balloons.

The power of children to redeem the mother's other-wise impoverished existence is the theme of several poems, which are set in the context of a mother bringing up her child alone. In 'By Candlelight' (*CP*, pp. 236–7) the mother dreads the sense of abandonment and neglect the child growing up without a father will inevitably have to face. She sits holding her child

32

in the candlelight, singing to him and rocking him. 'Nick and the Candlestick' (*CP*, pp. 240–2) takes up this theme, engendered by the fear which the mother feels for her child in a hostile and threatening world:

> Let the mercuric
> Atoms that cripple drip
> Into the terrible well,
>
> You are the one
> Solid the spaces lean on, envious.
> You are the baby in the barn.

The equation of the child with Christ – no blasphemy is intended, since the reference signifies the special place the child occupies in its mother's heart – recurs in the later poem 'Mary's Song' (*CP*, p. 257) and seems perfectly understandable in this context. The poem focuses on the terrible ambivalence of the world and the omnipresent violence in everyday life:

> It is a heart,
> This holocaust I walk in,
> O golden child the world will kill and eat.

Plath's writings about children are some of the most eloquent love poems of modern poetry. For example, 'Child' (*CP*, p. 265), written in the last month of her life:

> Your clear eye is the one absolutely beautiful thing,
> I want to fill it with color and ducks,
> The zoo of the new
>
> Whose names you meditate –
> April snowdrop, Indian pipe,
> Little

33

Stalk without wrinkle,
Pool in which images
Should be grand and classical

Not this troublous
Wringing of hands, this dark
Ceiling without a star.

Most of the poems she wrote on children are coloured by Plath's gentle, self-mocking sense of humour and her wanting to protect children against the dangers of an intrinsically violent and insane world. The relationship between mother and child is not one to be taken for granted, but the love and care a mother feels for her child is threatened by the violence inherent in the external patriarchal society.

Plath's poems on the theme of personal relations challenged the preconceptions of her time and with their honesty and seriousness they exposed both the dishonesty and destructiveness which lay behind the prevailing social mores. Far from being merely critical and destructive, they show how patriarchal society has made life threatening and counter-productive for men as well as women. Each relationship is shown to exist in struggle and relationships between women are drawn as difficult to achieve because of societal pressure and socialised passivity. Her poems show her to be very much a pioneer, with her angry rejection of insufficient and damaging personal relations. The brutality of patriarchal society, coupled with her candid eroticism and open confrontation with hypocrisy and the snares of gentility, link Plath to a great moralist tradition, embodied by her role-models Virginia Woolf and D H Lawrence, and make her work a very strong platform for writers who followed in her footsteps.

3. The Death Fallacy

A suicidal nature?

Since Plath's poetry defies simplistic interpretations, several critics have sought to understand what she is writing about by extrapolating from her life to the poetry. The initial attraction to her work arose specifically with the sensational and dramatic nature of her suicide at the age of 30 and with the publication of the *Ariel* collection, ending with its supposedly suicidal poems – 'Edge' and 'Words'. The biographical approach to Plath's work is, as has been shown, fraught with difficulties and distortions, so it would seem that to understand Plath's treatment of the theme of death another appraisal of her poetry has to be undertaken.

Conclusive proof of Plath's suicidal nature is seen by several critics, such as P R King and Edward Butscher[1] to lie in the arrangement of the poems in *Ariel*. Yet the selection of the poems in *Ariel*, which initially won Plath more notoriety than acclaim, was made and arranged by her literary executor, Ted Hughes, and this was not disclosed until publication of the *Collected Poems* in 1981, nearly 20 years after Plath died. Plath in fact intended, as can be seen in the note at the end of the *Collected Poems*, for *Ariel* to begin with the word 'Love' ('Morning Song') and to end with the word 'Spring' ('Wintering').[2] 'Suicidal' poems such as 'Edge' and 'Words' were to be held back for a later publication.

One of the most frequent charges levelled at Plath is that she regarded death as a means of rebirth and purification. Death on an individual and universal basis was indeed a theme which interested Plath, but there is no evidence in her work that it was a condition she aspired to.

One of her major critics, David Holbrook, believes that 'throughout her work there is a continual theme of "in the end is my beginning" – not in the Christian sense, but in ways in which the imagery shows that death offered her a rebirth.'[3] In his reading of 'The Arrival of the Bee Box' (*CP*, pp. 212–3), for example, he takes the poem's images to be those of 'a rebirth, beginning with a dead baby, ending with free bees, and the escape from death.'[4] There is, however, no textual evidence for the assumption that the poem begins with a 'dead baby'. In fact, the only oblique reference to a baby, made in jocular fashion, is the comparison of the receptacle in which the bees arrive to 'the coffin of a midget/Or a square baby'. Whether or not the poem closes with 'free bees' – and in fact it closes with the speaker's *proposal* to set them free – is irrelevant, since there is no reason for her (the speaker in each of the 'bee cycle' of poems appears to be female) to identify with them. In fact, if there is any justification for reading this poem to be one in which a rebirth occurs, it can only be a 'rebirth' attained through a clearer vision. The speaker ceases to imagine the bees as a threat to her existence, as 'a box of maniacs', and adopts a more healthy realistic perspective on the world around her.

Another poem taken by Holbrook to be a ritual of 'death-rebirth'[5] is 'Face Lift' (*CP*, pp. 155–6). This poem deals on one level with a cosmetic operation, a face-lift, but its underlying theme is that of regeneration. By sloughing off an older, more unsightly, layer the speaker in this poem experiences a spiritual and physical rebirth: 'Mother to myself, I wake swaddled in gauze,/Pink and smooth as a baby.'[6] The assertion of one side of the self over the other is not achieved through death, for the cast-off self is seen, wryly, as being very much alive: 'They've trapped her laboratory jar.'[7] This parody on the beauty is certainly concerned with a change of face, but, contrary to Holbrook's interpretation, the rebirth occurs not through death but through discarding one facet of the self – on one level, old facial skin, and on a deeper level, a redundant self, the self of a woman who lived as a caricature of a housewife, without her own identity. 'Broody and in long skirts on [her] first husband's sofa, . . .' The poem ends with the female speaker giving birth to herself, an image which feminist writers such as Adrienne Rich have made their own, to signify emancipation.

As a third example of his theory that Plath makes a 'search for birth through death', Holbrook cites the poem 'Lady Lazarus' (*CP*, pp. 244–7). To his mind, it 'declares raucously that the big strip-tease of death must be frequently repeated'.[8] Plath's own commentary, however, helps to clarify her intentions behind this poem: 'The speaker is a woman who has the great and terrible gift of being reborn. The only trouble is, she has to die first. She is the phoenix, the libertarian spirit, what you will. She is also just a good, plain, very resourceful woman.'[9] The poem takes place on primarily a metaphorical level. The speaker is 'the phoenix, the libertarian spirit', and, by implication, the deaths she dies are also metaphorical. The poem's primary intent is not to glorify some death-rebirth ritual, rather to indict an immoral consumer society which regards 'dying' as just another 'act' to be savoured.[10] The systematic self-destruction of the speaker is a titillating experience for the 'peanut-crunching crowd',[11] and it is this crowd, not the speaker or Plath, which wishes the perverse circus act to be repeated. The speaker is merely a performer who feels that she must excel in dying, just as she has been compelled to excel in everything else. She observes with considerable irony: 'Dying/Is an art, like everything else./I do it exceptionally well.'

Perhaps the most salient characteristic of this poem is the woman's determination to revenge herself on those responsible for her torture. This wish for revenge may express itself in terms of a rebirth: 'Out of the ash/I rise with my red hair'. The warning is that even when her tormentors think they have utterly exploited her, she will still have enough strength within her – being a 'plain resourceful woman' – to face life anew, and even to reverse the process, to 'eat men like air'. An equation of the 'suicidal' performance of Lady Lazarus with Plath's own suicide obscures the most important objective of the poem: to protest against the subjection of women by a consumer-oriented society run by men used to abusing their power.

The poem 'Getting There' (*CP*, pp. 247–9), one of Plath's most complex poems, is regarded by David Holbrook as additional proof of his hypothesis. He sees the poem as being about a spiritual journey embarked on by the speaker who 'seeks renewal in death'.[12] There is certainly a journey of sorts under-taken but it is focused into the world of nightmare – the female speaker is trapped in 'the straw of boxcars', like cattle on the way to the slaughterhouse or Jews *en route* for the concentration camp, and she feels herself doomed to die agonisingly slowly. 'How far is it?/How far is it now?' she asks repeatedly. Death seems a nightmarish inevitability; the speaker is horrified to find she cannot undo herself 'and the train is steaming'. The world is a violent backdrop; there are 'black muzzles/Revolving', 'wounded', 'thunder and guns'. Torn between two horrific alternatives, she longs for a 'still place/Turning and turning in the middle air,/Untouched and untouchable'. This place of refuge she desires belongs neither to death nor to life, and she wants to be able to reach it without having to undergo some drastic transformation. She hopes that there she will find some lasting security. Death, on the other hand, constitutes the ultimate waste of creative energy; it is a 'dewdrop', a 'bloodspot'. Resigned to death in sheer exhaustion, she tries to face it as dispassionately as possible, until she concentrates on the image of herself dead:

> The body of this woman,
> Charred skirts and deathmask
> Mourned by religious figures, by garlanded
>   children.

She decides that between her living self and this image there are too many 'obstacles' and 'The fire's between us'.[13] Death has receded as an option. So she resolves to clean up the mess both internally and externally: she '. . . shall bury the wounded like pupas' and '. . . shall count and bury the dead'.

Death no longer endangers her, for she is a survivor. The souls of the dead may 'writhe in a dew', but she has become impervious to harm, so they become 'incense' in her track, a sign of the miraculous transfiguration following her decision to live.

If the train can be regarded as a metaphor for the woman's life, which previously seemed destined for death, then the 'carriages' are stages in her life; as she acknowledges the possibility of a more active lifestyle and subsequent regeneration, 'the carriages rock, they are cradles.' At the end of the poem, the speaker is 'stepping from this skin/Of old bandages, boredoms, old faces', leaving behind a jaded, painful life. The 'Lethe', which endows her with the capacity to forget the shambles of the past and start afresh, untroubled by memories, seems to be something which is not attainable through death but which, on the contrary, only the living can have access to.[14] 'Getting There'[15] is about a rebirth or regeneration of sorts – the speaker does after all arrive at a destination[16] – but it is not a rebirth which occurs through death.

In the view of one critic, Annette Lavers, Sylvia Plath thought that 'purification can be achieved in death, in which the scattered personality is seen as gradually withdrawing its tainted externals', as in 'Fever 103°', in 'Tulips' and in 'Paralytic'.[17] It is true that death does at times appear initially to be a way of attaining a purer and more bearable existence. This is particularly relevant with regard to 'A Birthday Present' (*CP*, pp. 206–8), a poem of despair and disillusionment about the failure of a relationship. The speaker longs to leave a sordid life of abuse behind her, imagining death as being 'Pure and clean as the cry of a baby'. However, it is not at all typical; in any event the core subject-matter of the poem is the end of a relationship and betrayal – it is not fundamentally concerned with the expression of a death-wish. Lavers' hypothesis does not however hold for the three poems she specifically refers to. While it is possible to interpret 'Paralytic' (*CP*, pp. 266–7) and 'Fever 103°' as poems in which the speaker appears to desire purification through death, it is important to take into account the nature of the speaker in each poem before concluding that Plath herself endorsed this attitude.

Irony and parody

In 'Paralytic' the speaker is severely criticised for his narcissistic self-absorption and likened to the 'The claw/Of the magnolia,/Drunk on its own scents' which 'asks nothing of life'. He lies passively taking

in the days, incapable of relating to his daughters or
his wife:

> My wife, dead and flat, in 1920 furs,
> Mouth full of pearls,
>
> Two girls
> As flat as she, who whisper 'We're your daughters'.

The poem is not about the abandoning of tainted
externals, but rather the condemnation of someone
who is obsessively concerned with his own internal
state: 'I smile, a buddha, all/Wants, desire/Falling
from me like rings/Hugging their lights.' Similarly,
there is a kind of purification through death, aspired
to and apparently attained, in 'Fever 103°',[18] but it is
not one which Plath sets as an example. Here, as in
'Paralytic', the speaker is sick and does not look to
life to cure this sickness. She has a high fever and,
with it, the delirium which makes her both see the
world as intrinsically evil and also equate the 'bodies
of adulterers' with her own and her lover's: 'The
sheets grow heavy as a lecher's kiss.' She wishes
for stasis, for a time when she can stop flickering,
'off, on, off, on' in pain.[19] Her wish to escape her
physical reality is motivated mainly by her inability
to bear contamination, or what she, in her illness,
considers as such: 'your body/Hurts me as the world
hurts God . . .' In this state she sees her illness as
being the direct result of sexual intimacy with her
partner and she desires to become virginal again.
Life, which is equated with suffering, is rejected
and she assumes what can best be described as a
machine-like purity which will, she believes, guide
her away from 'The tongues of hell' into 'Paradise'.
The wry humour pervading this poem make it very
obvious that Plath is parodying the ideal of purity in

religion and relationship, and that it is purity and not death which is its central target.

In the poem 'Tulips' (*CP*, pp. 160–2) a conflict between life and death occurs, ultimately tending towards an acceptance of life, in spite of the suffering this entails.[20] As a result of illness: 'I have given my name and my day-clothes up to the nurses/And my history to the anaesthetist and my body to surgeons' – the female speaker, 'learning peacefulness', has withdrawn from normal existence to become 'nobody', 'a nun', purified: 'I have never been so pure.' This 'peacefulness' is a state akin to death: 'It is what the dead close on, finally; I imagine them/Shutting their mouths on it, like a Communion tablet.' The speaker, with no identity left, seems to be lapsing into death, but the presence of flowers in the room revives her zest for life: 'Their redness talks to my wound, it corresponds.' The intensity of their colour, the colour of the 'red/Eye' – the creative force – of 'Ariel' (*CP*, pp. 239–40) reminds the speaker of her own vitality and she begins to doubt the value of her purified state. Becoming aware of her situation, she sees herself in her passive state as '. . . flat, ridiculous, a cut-paper shadow/between the eye of the sun and the eyes of the tulips.' She is stricken with guilt, as she realises how, between these two vital forces she has tried to deny her own self: 'And I have no face, I have wanted to efface myself.' The tulips,[21] moving gently in the air currents, constitute the focal point of her environment: 'They concentrate my attention, that was happy/Playing and resting without committing itself.' The room that was 'winter', 'snowed-in' seems to her to be 'warming' to the exotic tulips, which are '. . . opening like the mouth of some great African cat . . .' Identifying with the tulips in their spontaneous vitality, she regains an awareness of her heart that '. . . opens and closes/Its bowl of red blooms out of sheer

42

love of me.' Instead of withdrawing from the world into the rarefied mechanical state of death as in 'Fever 103°', the speaker in 'Tulips' regains her attachment to life through a Lawrentian appreciation of an intensity and beauty which correspond to her own.

Joyce Carol Oates has said about Plath that 'she understood well the hellish fate of being Swift's true counterpart, the woman who agrees that the physical side of life is a horror, an ungainly synthesis of flesh and spirit.'[22] While this may be an accurate description of the sick woman in 'Paralytic' and 'Fever 103°' it is, however, not applicable to 'Tulips', which, devoid of irony, seems to put forward Plath's own attitude. It is because of the speaker's heightened awareness of the tulips and her own physical beauty that she has been reborn – in the sense of making a new commitment to her life. In the majority of Plath's poems there is a conflict between life and death and, except for the few poems of complete disillusionment, the choice is emphatically for life.

The theme of death as a means of reintegration in nature pervades 'I am Vertical' (*CP*, p. 162) and 'Last Words' (*CP*, p. 172). 'I am Vertical' seems to be an expression of the death-wish as formulated by Freud.[23] The reasons why the speaker in this poem desires death have been influenced by her sense of alienation; she is at odds with the world around her. She would like to be 'in open conversation' with the sky, since this would make her 'useful'. In death, she imagines, reintegration with the natural environment will occur: 'Then the trees may touch me for once, and the flowers have time for me.' Prompting this wish for stasis is her apparent dissatisfaction with the life of the intellect,[24] for it is her mind that makes her painfully aware of the transience of human life. This motivates her desire to be similar to the Lethe-like flowers and trees: 'Thoughts gone dim.' It is important to note that the dissatisfaction which the speaker feels with her life does not give rise to any overt suicidal tendencies. Death may seem in some way attractive, but the speaker is in no rush to find out if the appearance matches up to the reality.

The situation in 'Last Words' is somewhat similar. 'I do not trust the spirit', the speaker says. '. . . It escapes like steam/In dreams, through mouth-hole or eye-hole. I can't stop it./One day it won't come back.' In contrast, inanimate objects seem to possess a well-defined permanence, and the speaker imagines that even her disembodied state after death will be pleasant because of the identity which her familiar cooking utensils and cosmetics, to be buried with her according to Egyptian custom, will afford her: 'the shine of these small things' is for her 'sweeter than the face of Ishtar.' In contrast to 'I am Vertical' the speaker in this poem still treasures her human identity; death here is not envisaged as more desirable than life. In this poem Plath is gently mocking burial rituals and the tone is tongue-in-cheek.

Apart from these two poems in which death, not without considerable irony, is imagined as a way to peace or reintegration with the environment, death appears horrific in Plath's work.

The horror of death

In 'Two Views of a Cadaver Room' (*CP*, p. 114) the gross squalor of death is deliberately juxtaposed against the frail beauty of life. The first section in the 'dissecting room' sets the scene.[25] An anatomy lesson is in progress and the procedure is characterised by the scientific, impersonal approach of the students to the human corpses they are dissecting. Since the corpses resemble anything but human beings – they are 'black as burnt turkey', a 'rubble of skull plates and old leather', with even the dead foetuses 'snail-nosed' – this unemotional attitude seems at first to be the speaker's valid response until her medical student friend hands her 'the cut-out heart like a cracked heirloom'. The heart is a powerful symbol throughout Plath's work: 'a bowl of red blooms', the speaker's perception of it saves her from death in 'Tulips'; likewise, her recognition of it here as an 'heirloom' makes it impossible for her to maintain an impersonal attitude towards death. Consequently, in contrast to, and in defiance of, this process of dehumanisation, the second section of the poem shows life in its most passionate and vital form. The speaker remembers a painting by Breughel, 'The Triumph of Death', 'of smoke and slaughter', in which only two lovers are 'blind to the carrion army', and 'deaf to the fiddle in the hands/Of the death's head shadowing their song'. The lovers are valued all the more for their frail mortality: they '. . . flourish; not for long.' But they are saved from the overwhelmingly nightmarish impact of death, because of their absorption in love and life: 'Yet desolation, stalled in paint, spares the little country/Foolish, delicate, in the lower right hand corner.' And it is this unequivocal commitment to life which excites the envy and admiration of the speaker in this poem.

Margaret Newlin has put forward the idea that in Plath's work 'Always death is noble, Greek in stature, eschewing the humiliating tubes and leftover wine, the drooling mouth and the green discoloration'.[26] This theory is, however, only applicable to a few poems, and only when Plath chooses to mock or criticise the speaker or the situation; it does not hold good for a serious study on the subject, as can be seen from a study of three commonly misinterpreted poems: 'Berck-Plage' (*CP*, pp. 196–201), 'Death & Co.' (*CP*, p. 254) and 'Edge' (*CP*, pp. 272–3).

'Berck-Plage' focuses on two at first sight seemingly disconnected events, which are, in fact, related by virtue of their nightmarish content, a visit to a beach beside a home for the physically handicapped and the death and funeral of an old man.[27] As Ted Hughes's note to the poem explains, Berck-Plage was 'a beach on the coast of Normandy, which SP visited in June 1961. Overlooking the sea there was a large hospital for mutilated war veterans and accident victims who took their exercise along the sands.'[28]

At first it seems as if death had made an improvement on the old man's condition. The speaker observes: 'How superior he is now./It is like possessing a saint./The nurses in their wing-caps are no longer so beautiful.' Then, as his bed is moved, she has a better view of the corpse and is appalled at what she sees: 'This is what it is to be complete. It is horrible.' In death, the old man appears inhuman, birdlike: 'his powdery beak/Rises so whitely unbuffeted'. Despite the mesmerising appeal of the funeral ceremony – the coffin is '. . . like a beautiful woman,/A crest of breasts, eyelids and lips' while the children marvel at the curious procession of the pallbearers bearing 'a wonderful thing', (the wonder underscored by the powerful slow-motion technique employed by Plath: the speaker is 'Gliding up in low gear behind the cart.'; . . . the children/Smell the melt of shoe-blacking,/Their faces turning, wordless and slow,/Their eyes opening/On a wonderful thing') – it cannot belie the horrifying bleakness of death. The burial, like the rest of what is related, is surrealistic and terrifying: the grave is 'a naked mouth, red and awkward.' There is no reprieve from the grim finality of death: 'For a minute the sky pours into the hole like plasma./There is no hope, it is given up.' There is no nobility here.

In 'Death & Co.' death has been stripped of the last

element of romance. Like everything else in modern society it has become impersonal, comparable to some kind of perverse business deal. In her own commentary on this poem Plath said that 'This poem . . . is about the double or schizophrenic nature of death – the marmoreal coldness of Blake's death mask, say, hand in glove with the fearful softness of worms, water, and other catabolisms. I imagine these two aspects of death as two men, two business friends, who have come to call.'[29] The first of the two faces, exhibiting 'The nude/Verdigris of the condor', tries to seduce the speaker into believing that death brings perfection of the human condition:

> He tells me how sweet
> The babies look in their hospital
> Icebox, a simple
>
> Frill at the neck,
> Then the flutings of their Ionian
> Death-gowns,
> Then two little feet.

His approach is a serious one: 'He does not smile or smoke.' He works by negation, his means of persuasion dependent on making the speaker regard her life and work as a failure: 'He tells me how badly I photograph.' The other face of death uses a more sexual approach: 'He wants to be loved.' Oozing falsity, he smiles, and his hair is 'long and plausive'; he is a 'Bastard/Masturbating a glitter'. The idea here is that suicide can be an orgasmic experience. In Plath's work orgasm is usually synonymous with the release of creative energy,[30] however in this poem the orgasm is merely a self-indulgent, obscene act of narcissism and the denial of art.

M L Rosenthal has suggested that the last line

'Somebody's done for' is a 'vision of the speaker's own death.'[31] Taking the last two lines of the poem, 'The frost makes a flower,/The dew makes a star', as a characterisation of the two faces of death, it appears almost as if the speaker has succumbed, however horrific the fate seemed to her, since to be 'done for' hardly seems to be an attractive proposition.[32] Yet this is too superficial a conclusion as it fails to take into account the irony and sardonic tone of the poem. Both faces of death seem incredibly camp and are suitably mocked by Plath, and the idiom of the poem is particularly melodramatic, much like a parody of a horror film or *film noir*. It is also highly unlikely that Plath would agree with that which she mocks so successfully.

The poem 'Edge' has been regarded by numerous critics as an instance of the death instinct, which according to Freud was an urge to self-destruction. Indeed, David Holbrook considers it an 'idolization of suicide and infanticide.'[33] This interpretation seems to spring more from an attempt to equate Plath's suicide with her handling of the theme of death, and it fails to take into account the obvious detachment, indicated by the biting irony, of the writer. Perfection, the central theme of 'Edge'[34] entails the woman reclaiming all her parts, which in her eyes also include her children. She

. . . has folded

Them back into her body as petals
Of a rose close when the garden

Stiffens and odours bleed
From the sweet, deep throats of the night flower.

But this type of perfection is the target of the speaker's irony and, by implication, Plath's as well.

The woman's suicide and infanticide are condemned as 'The illusion of a Greek necessity'; her act a shoddy pretence of an idealistic heroic act. The description of the dead woman's children as being each 'a white serpent', is further at odds with the treatment of children elsewhere in Plath's work.[35] Significantly, the dead woman's body 'wears the smile of accomplishment.' Smiles often denote evil in Plath, and the dead woman here is in no way depicted as a heroine. In fact she seems the opposite of any character depicted positively by Plath, as, for example, the wife/First Voice in 'Three Women', who gives birth and exclaims 'I accomplish a work'. In contrast, the woman in 'Edge' wears only the 'smile of accomplishment'. A reading of this poem which does not take into account Plath's considerable use of irony fails to do it justice.

Plath's love of life

Plath was not obsessed with death, neither was she attracted to suicide as three poems, written during the last week of her life, make clear. 'Years' (*CP*, pp. 255–6), 'Totem' (*CP*, pp. 264–5) and 'Words' (*CP*, p. 270) show that Plath's positive attitude towards life remained constant and that to the end death continued to appear to be a grim and horrific fate.

In 'Years' the speaker voices her distaste of immortality: 'Eternity bores me,/I never wanted it.' In contrast to the emptiness, the 'vacuous black' it embodies, she loves 'the piston in motion' and the 'hooves of the horses' – life and passion.

The speaker in 'Totem' suffers from a painful awareness of her own mortality: 'The engine is killing the track, the track is silver,/It stretches into the distance. It will be eaten nevertheless.' Death

49

is clearly a horrific prospect and it becomes all the more hideous in proportion to the consciousness of its victims. The uncertainty of the existence of a benevolent God suggests the idea that the afterlife can be as terrifying as death itself. If indeed, a God exists, it seems more probable that he is malevolent, enjoying a sadistic pleasure in having human beings:

> . . . buzz like blue children
> In nets of the infinite,
>
> Roped in at the end by the one
> Death with its many sticks.

With the horrific absurdity of death the only defence is a wholehearted commitment to life. But this commitment is much more than merely a last-minute measure to ward off the idea of death. The speaker in 'Totem' is in love with life: 'The world is blood-hot and personal' infinitely valuable. Its beauty lies in its variability. Life is 'no terminus', instead it is a series of opportunities for expansion: '. . . suitcases/Out of which the same self unfolds like a suit/Bald and shiny, with pockets of wishes'.

The horror of death is also the subject of 'Words'. In this poem the speaker reflects on her own death, decreed by the 'fixed stars' which 'Govern a life', the powers that represent and exult in stasis and passivity. Against the ominousness of death the speaker finds consolation not only in a keen appreciation of the beauty of her surroundings but also in the knowledge that her writing will help her to transcend the limits imposed on her life and thereby achieve some kind of immortality. Her art is regarded as an extension of all that is good in life; it is a lasting reincarnation of the life-force:

50

Axes
After whose stroke the wood rings,
And the echoes!
Echoes travelling
Off from the centre like horses.

and as the poem ends, the immortality of art – 'Words dry and riderless,/The indefatigable hoof-taps' – is the element that redeems the speaker's own mortality.

Plath lived for much of her life under the burden of having to live up to her own exceptionally high standards. While she was at times depressed and ended her own life, it is nonetheless abundantly evident that it is life and not death which is celebrated in her work. Nowhere is there anything even remotely resembling a paean to death; the subject is always treated negatively and associated with the corruption she believed inherent in a decadent society.

The central theme in Plath's work, as in her own life, was the constant struggle for active, positive life, set against the passive resignation of death – whether physical or its attitudinal equivalent.

The fact that Sylvia Plath personally lost the struggle for life cannot detract from the success she achieved in her work which indicated the power and ultimate triumph of life over death.

4. Subverting Stereotypes

Plath's interest in religion and the afterlife was, like her interest in personal relations, in line with 'acceptable' subject-matter for a woman poet.[1] Religion had been a key theme for her contemporaries, the Confessional Poets, as it had been for those poets who had a strong influence on her work, such as D H Lawrence, Emily Dickinson, T S Eliot and W B Yeats. However, just as Plath had sought to demythologise personal relations in a restrictive patriarchal context,[2] so too in her writing on religion and the afterlife she confronted and deflated a falsifying and deadly ideology. Plath's exploration of this topic also reinforced her belief in existentialism as the most honest and all-embracing way to live.

Her concern with the theme of religion was partially derived from her family background. Her father had trained to be a Lutheran minister, and for several years her mother had taught Sunday school. In 1955 at the start of her writing career, Plath defined herself as '. . . not really a Christian in the true sense of the word, but more of an ethical culturist: labels don't matter . . .'[3] Even so, in 1962 she started attending her local Anglican church in the small Devon village she lived in. She was highly critical of the rector's religious bigotry, which she found symptomatic of the Christian religion; as she wrote to her mother:

> . . . I honestly dislike, or rather, scorn the rector. I told you about his ghastly H-Bomb sermon, didn't I, where he said this was the happy prospect of the Second Coming and how lucky we Christians were compared to the stupid pacifists and humanists and 'educated pagans' who feared being incinerated,

etc. etc. I have not been to church since. I felt it was a sin to support such insanity even by my presence.[4]

And she stressed in the same letter how strongly she felt about Unitarianism,[5] the religion she had been brought up in:

Marcia Plumer sent me a copy of a wonderful sermon on fallout shelters by her local Unitarian minister, which made me weep. I'd really be a church-goer if I was back in Wellesley . . . the Unitarian church is my church. How I miss it![6]

Anxious that her children grow up with some form of religious background, Plath wrote later that year of her intention to take Frieda and Nick to church in London[7] and Frieda to Sunday school:

I'm sure as she starts thinking for herself, she will drift away from the church, but I know how incredibly powerful the words of that little Christian prayer, 'God is my help in every need', which you taught us has been at odd moments of my life, so think it will do her good to feel part of this spiritual community.[8]

Towards the end of her life Plath corresponded regularly with a young Jesuit priest studying literature at Oxford, who had written her a fan letter.[9] The question of religion remained a burning issue for her throughout her life.

God's indifference and cruelty

Strongly influenced by Unitarian teaching, Plath found the idea of the Holy Trinity hard to swallow.

The intellectual abstractness of the figure-heads of conventional religion failed to satisfy her spiritual needs. In her poetry Plath showed how the figures of the Trinity were too far removed from everyday reality for human beings to believe in. She regarded them as an invention by men, intent on maintaining supremacy, even in spiritual matters, over women. She was convinced that 'the Trinity was a male plot to replace the mother in the normal family unit with a vague spirit, the Holy Ghost'.[10]

Religion and the question of life after death have long been popular subjects for all poets, but there is a great difference in the treatment of these themes by male and female American writers. As one critic, Emily Stipe Watts, has noted, in comparison to their male colleagues, American women poets seem strangely distant from God.[11] Plath's handling of the theme of religion showed her attempt yet again to deflate a series of myths confining and restricting the identity of women.

The two primary traits Plath ascribed to the Christian God were wilful indifference and sadistic cruelty. Nietzsche's idea of the absent God held good whenever contact was attempted; likewise, the severity of human life and the horrific climax of death suggested a sadistic nature in the God which had created human beings for some unfathomable reason and then abandoned them to the terrifying absurdity of their existence.[12]

In the verse drama 'Three Women' (*CP*, pp. 176–87) the secretary who has the miscarriage characterises God the Father and Son as 'flat':

I see the Father conversing with the Son.
Such flatness cannot but be holy,
'Let us make a heaven,' they say.

54

'Let us flatten and launder the grossness from
   these souls.'

The verb 'flatten' implies that entry to the one-
dimensional Christian heaven requires a violent
reduction of personality. Even if humans thereby
lose their grossness, one of their obviously less
redeemable characteristics (and in this and other
poems it is left open as to whether this is in fact
a negative characteristic[13]), they will have to lose
their three-dimensionality/humanity in the process.
Redemption under these conditions resembles the
type of activity operating in the laundromat.
   Even where redemption is not a matter of God's
chilling indifference to human needs, it has overwhelmingly negative connotations. In 'Brasilia'[14]
(*CP*, pp. 258–9) the speaker fears for the defor-
mation of her baby which his spiritual redemption
would seem to imply: 'And my baby a nail/Driven,
driven in.' The angels, heralds of redemption and the
companions of God, are depicted as mindless and
mechanical phenomena:

   . . . people with torsos of steel
   Winged elbows and eyeholes

   Awaiting masses
   Of cloud to give them expression

'Super-people' they are not. Plath regards their state
as nothing worth striving for; she finds human life
much more attractive, 'Red earth, motherly blood,'
in comparison to redemption by a demonic God who
eats 'People like light rays'. Such an afterlife would be
a travesty of a painful yet beautiful human existence.
Accordingly, the speaker begs God, who would
appear to be a combination of God as portrayed
in the Old Testament combined with some science

55

fiction monster, to spare her child the horror of such an infernal afterlife:

> . . . leave
> This one
> Mirror safe, unredeemed
>
> By the dove's annihilation,
> The glory,
> The power, the glory.[15]

For Plath the Old Testament God is either brutal in his ways or indifferent.

Several poems focus on the concept of the absent God. In 'Lyonesse'[16] (*CP*, pp. 233–4) he is 'the big God', unsympathetic and aloof, who has let the fertile kingdom be submerged by the sea. His failure to save it is attributable to apathy, a lack of concern amounting to laziness: he had 'lazily closed one eye.' The reverse side of his nature is savagery: he appears like a vicious 'animal/In his cage of ether, his cage of stars.' The final view of such a deity is appropriately pessimistic: 'The white gape of his mind was the real Tabula Rasa.' On another level the poem deals with the subject of betrayal. The Lyonians' idea of heaven was that it would be an extension of their present existence. But their drowning is a loss of life. Plath uses this mythical allusion to show how unreliable and dangerous is an attachment to a belief in the afterlife.

This idea of a demonic, sadistic deity, the 'Herr God, Herr Lucifer' of 'Lady Lazarus' (*CP*, pp. 244–7) reappears in one of Plath's last poems, 'Totem' (*CP*, pp. 264–5). Here, as Annette Lavers has commented, there is a 'revolt against the deity, which is shown as a bloodthirsty pagan idol, grimacing like a skull, and at the same time mobile like a scarecrow, and ridiculous and counterfeit, like it.'[17] In this poem Christ is allied with Plato, and the affinity of this figure-head with the world of abstractions and his detachment from ordinary life is stressed. These two are 'the people that were important' with 'Their round eyes, their teeth, their grimaces/On a stick that rattles and clicks, a counterfeit snake.' Here, the components of nightmare are compounded with the absurdity of burlesque. So God becomes a spider – 'I am mad, calls the spider, waving its many arms' – while human beings are 'flies' who 'buzz like blue children/In nets of the infinite.' The relationship between God and his creatures is likened to that between a hunter and his prey. Without doubt this is the most horrific view of God to be found anywhere in Plath's work, and significantly it is one which was the result of her attempt to come to terms with the traditional, abstract figure-heads of Christianity, which Plath frequently deflates and shows to be inadequate.

Plath's view of the figure-heads of religion may be seen to have been in part inspired by images of father and mother. There is evidence in several poems that Plath's essentially negative view of God was coloured by her unresolved relationship with her father, who died when she was aged 8. He is the godlike figure in 'Full Fathom Five' (*CP*, pp. 92–3) ('You defy questions;/You defy other godhood' the speaker accuses him) whose death has caused the speaker to be exiled from his kingdom: 'I walk dry on your kingdom's border/Exiled to no good.'

In 'Berck-Plage' (*CP*, pp. 196–201) the '. . . high, dead, toeless foot of this priest' can be taken as a reference to Plath's father's amputation, carried out in a last desperate attempt to save his life. Significantly, in the first section of the poem the speaker remarks: 'Is it any wonder he affects a black cassock?'; the uniform does not make him into a real priest. The most direct equation of God with the father[18] comes in the poem 'Daddy' (*CP*, pp. 222–4), in which he is initially described as 'Marble-heavy, a bag full of God', only to be ritually stripped of his godlike status: 'Not God but a swastika.' The father (and by extension patriarchal society), who has caused his daughter to suffer torture and almost death in the poem, is not on a par with the immense power of God, a power which Plath implies is used only negatively; he can only symbolise, not incorporate, evil.

Too good to be true

The New Testament concept of Christ appears, by virtue of his adopted humanity, to be a more conciliatory figure than the remote, austere and entirely divine God the Father of the Old Testament. Yet Plath highlights the horrific contradictions in the characterisation of Christ. In the poem 'I Want, I Want' (*CP*, p. 106), based on an infant's incessant cries for attention and satisfaction, the 'Baby god', synonymous with Christ, is 'immense, bald' and his father has 'Raised his men of skin and bone' as 'Barbs on the crown of gilded wire,/Thorns on the bloody rose-stem.' Christ's death on the cross appears not as a sacrifice for the salvation of humanity, but rather as an egocentric act, for which the human community and not Christ will have to suffer. This is no God of mercy that respects and offers succour to the suffering; it is one that is intent on ignoring or even persecuting humanity. And it is significant that the infant's cries are unheeded, his satisfactions are unmet – images of dryness abound throughout the poem ('The dry volcanoes cracked and spit,/Sand abraded the milkless lip'). Without the influence of women and a real mother, Christ, Plath suggests, is endowed with only negative potential and is essentially a sterile, destructive figure.

Plath's depiction of the Virgin Mary can be said to have been influenced by her own complex relationship to her mother, to which 'Medusa' (*CP*, pp. 224–6) can be seen in part as a reference. In this poem the female speaker asks her female tormentor: 'Who do you think you are?/A communion wafer? Blubbery Mary?'

The Virgin Mary has traditionally been regarded as the most appealing figure in Catholic mythology and has been depicted so favourably that the notion of a compassionate mediator with God has been jealously coveted by liberal Protestants. Endowed with maternal attributes and embodying both the Mother of God and the entire human race, the figure of Mary has, for Catholics, assumed an almost more important role than Christ. Plath's poetry, however, shows that the way Mary's character has been depicted in traditional religion has been too abstract and shallow to inspire confidence.

In her interpretation of Mary, Plath foreshadows feminist theory. As Phyllis Chesler has commented:

> Her only contact with divinity is through her 'servicing' of men: be it the Holy Father or her own son. Catholic mythology, as shown in Fra Bartholommeo's painting, symbolizes the enforced splitting of woman into either mother or whore – both of whom nurture, worship, and ultimately mourn a dead man and/or a divine male infant. Like many women, Mary foregoes sexual pleasure, physical prowess, and economic and intellectual power in order to become a 'mother'.[19]

Plath depicts Mary in 'Finisterre' (*CP*, pp. 169–70) as a cold and distant figure, a statue, 'Our Lady of the Shipwrecked', 'striding toward the horizon' in skirts of 'marble'; at her foot 'A marble sailor kneels . . . distractedly, and at his foot/A peasant woman in black/Is praying to the monument of the sailor praying.' An unlikely statue to worship, since it represents aloofness and self-importance, this act of devotion casts considerable doubt on the efficacy of the woman's prayer, directed towards an aloof and arrogant figure, who seems totally unconcerned with supplicants. In fact they appear too menial to merit her attention. 'Three times life size', she is, in fact, too good to be true – only a statue after all – and incapable of providing comfort.

Mary is attributed the qualities of remoteness and neglect by the mother/wife in the verse drama 'Three Women': 'dusk hoods me in blue now like a Mary./O colour of distance and forgetfulness!' The only exception to the portrayal of Mary as a detached, unconcerned abstraction is 'Mary's Song' (*CP*, p. 257). It is an exception because in this poem Mary is portrayed as primarily human, on a par with the rest of humankind and subject to the same fears, powerlessness and suffering. At the same time this reduction in stature deprives her of special powers; she is helpless to prevent suffering, in particular the suffering and crucifixion of her own son. She is therefore no source of consolation or protector of humans. Like the rest of humanity, Mary can only fear for her child exposed to the terrible ambivalence of the world: 'It is a heart/This holocaust I walk in,/O golden child the world will kill and eat.'

God's followers

Plath's examination of Christianity's major figureheads led her to the conclusion that God was essentially malevolent and Mary indifferent or powerless to do anything about the human plight. The followers of Christianity were viewed with equal suspicion.

In 'Magi' (*CP*, p. 148), the three wise men who come bearing gifts for the infant Christ are described with acute cynicism as: 'The real thing, all right: the Good, the True-/Salutary and pure as boiled water,/Loveless as the multiplication table.' Their unattractiveness stems from the same source as the flatness of the souls of the elect in 'Three Women.' They are, it is intimated, after the wrong star, seeking the wrong kind of God: 'They want the crib of some lamp-headed Plato'; an intellectual, not a baby,[20] and certainly not a baby girl, which is what they have got in the poem. Plath stresses women's abhorrence of such arid abstractions: 'What girl ever flourished in such company?' Plath's existential appreciation of life becomes very evident here: the reality of human life, in all its primitiveness, is infinitely preferable to the purified, grotesque state of the Christian elect. Christians in fact are depicted as a malevolent bunch. Acting in the name of their God, they indulge in activities more readily attributable to Satanists. Plath condemns them for 'Melting the tallow heretics'[21] ('Mary's Song', *CP*, p. 257).

The irony of the contradiction between professed Christian beliefs of compassion and forgiveness and the actual bloody history of Christianity did not escape Plath's attention. Accordingly, the ministers of Christianity come in for considerable criticism. Plath's views seem to a certain degree coloured by the fact that conventional religion was a mechanism for upholding a male hierarchy.[22] She censures the 'untidy lady revivalist' in 'On Deck' (*CP*, pp. 142–3), but in a way that is comparatively light-hearted. Plath ridicules the woman's character – she revels in materialism yet still professes to be morally superior to the lost souls in Berlin whom she plans to 'save'. Much more severe is Plath's depiction of the male ministers of God. In 'Berck-Plage' the priest casts a shoddy, tainted figure: '. . . the priest is a vessel,/A tarred fabric, sorry and dull.' The contact which the lady revivalist and the priest presumably have with God has not transformed them in any way, or if it has – and the priest is merely a 'vessel' – it has definitely not been for the best.

The importance of what is

Plath's poems show that she was very much preoccupied with the question of an afterlife, particularly towards the end of her life. Since her expectations of herself were so high, they could never be satisfied, and she needed something else to believe in.[23]

The need to have faith in something is the motif of the poem which constitutes her most explicit and definitive stance on God and Christianity – 'The Moon and the Yew Tree' (*CP*, pp. 172–3). In this poem a woman stands in the moonlight in a churchyard, trying to rationalise some meaning in to her life: 'I simply cannot see where there is to get to.' She stands on this full moon night, separated from her 'house' (her soul) by the 'headstones', the ultimate symbol of mortality. Out in the churchyard the 'grasses unload their griefs on my feet', an echo of an earlier poem 'Private Ground' (*CP*, pp. 130–1), where '. . . In here, the grasses/Unload their griefs on my shoes.'

In 'The Moon and the Yew Tree' the woman in her bare feet who feels the wetness of the grass, and who seems almost witch-like in what could easily be a meeting-place for some pagan ritual,[24] has a most intimate contact with nature, while there is a complete absence of communication between her and any higher being. In relation to her surroundings, the woman might as well be God, the grasses 'prickling my ankles and murmuring of their humility.' The yew tree points up, but instead of indicating the presence of a higher existence, it points only to the moon, which is 'no door'. The 'Gothic shape' of the yew tree, a naturalistic cathedral, highlights the moon as the most vivid aspect of the landscape. It is, as the speaker says, 'my mother'. She recognises that she is in some kind of relationship, a kinship with the moon, signifying the Muse, a kinship which helps to define her and provide a sense of identity. Even so, she craves the extra reassurance of religion:

> How I would like to believe in tenderness –
> The face of the effigy, gentled by candles,
> Bending, on me in particular, its mild eyes.

She knows, however, that this is a sham. The church provides no security; there is only shallow ritual, the ringing of bells 'Twice on Sunday', a ringing at odds with the environment: the bells 'startle the sky'. Their effect is even at variance with their purpose; they are 'Eight great tongues affirming the Resurrection', yet their sound does not refer to the resurrected Christ, but is merely an arrogant act of self-definition. No belief in God is inspired here; far from being conducive to spiritual enlightenment, the bells are crude artifices; they merely 'bong out' their names. Neither does the interior of the church, supposedly the dwelling-place of God, show evidence of any higher being; it is a place of statues, bearing no relation to life; they have 'hands and faces stiff with holiness'. The poem serves to underscore the hypocrisy and rigidity of some of the major exponents of Christianity. Its end dispenses with the notion of an afterlife: '. . . the message of the yew tree is blackness – blackness and silence.'[25] The bleakness of this relationship is tempered by the dominant presence of the moon, which '. . . sees nothing of this. She is bald and wild', impervious to the fears and sense of limitation felt by the speaker.

In spite of the failure of conventional religion to furnish proof of an afterlife, it nevertheless remained an important concern for Plath throughout her life and work.

Uncertainties

The poem 'Apprehensions' (*CP*, pp. 195–6) is one of a number of poems centred on the uncertainty of life after death, uncertainty which derives from an overly analytical, rationalist perspective. In this poem, which has no immediate religious frame of reference, the speaker describes herself in terms of walls, to which she initially ascribes the colour 'white' (in Plath's system of colours meaning indeterminate). The speaker finds the influence of the mind restrictive: 'Is there no way out of the mind?' she asks. Because of it the wall becomes 'A grey wall now, clawed and bloody'. The world of the intellect is far from idyllic: 'There are no trees or birds in this world,/There is only a sourness.'[26] She next envisages herself as a 'red wall' wincing continually, 'A red fist, opening and closing'. 'A red fist' is what she calls her heart, the choice of words showing that she is persisting in defiance of something or someone. She confesses to a horror of death: 'Of being wheeled off under crosses and a rain of pietas.'[27]

In 'Apprehensions', to dread the 'pietas' means to dread a Christian burial. The ceremony is meaningless because the speaker cannot believe in the afterlife it signifies. Envisaging her own death, she sees herself as a 'black wall', with unidentifiable birds perched on it. Like the angels in 'Brasilia' they react in a grotesque, mechanical fashion: they 'Swivel their

64

heads.' But they are no heralds proclaiming the resurrection of the speaker: 'There is no talk of immortality among these!' The final scene in the title: 'Cold blanks approach us.' And the advent of death is imminent and menacing: 'They move in a hurry.' 'Apprehensions' is ultimately nihilistic.[28] Its rationalisation of the question of an afterlife leads only to an unresolvable angst.

Similarly, the message of 'Years' (*CP*, pp. 255–6) is that life after death is a bleak form of stasis – the type of paralysing stasis the speaker/protagonist escaped from in 'Ariel' – while what the speaker treasures is 'The piston in motion – /My soul dies before it' and she continues defiantly on with the business of life: 'The hooves will not have it,/In blue distance the pistons hiss.' The central theme of this poem is that the only kind of life worth having is the business of life as it goes on in its routine, from day to day, from year to year, not the 'great Stasis' offered by the Christian concept of heaven. The years of the speaker's life, which 'enter as animals' are what is real for her, not the picturebook illusion of an unwanted passive existence: '. . . vacuous black,/Stars stuck all over, bright stupid confetti'. The repetition of the consonant 's' throughout the poem conveys the notion of energy in motion, and, through the sibilance, a dislike of the idea of eternity proposed by Christianity.

Existential beliefs

One positive recognition to be gleaned from Plath's study of traditional religion and the afterlife is the welcome acceptance of life in the here and now, a life of creativity. For Plath this reality was influenced by her mysticism[29] and also by what towards the end of her life amounted to an existential attitude towards life.[30] She was conversant with the work of

Camus and Sartre,[31] and her MA thesis had been on the work of Dostoevsky, the greatest exponent of existentialism in the nineteenth century. In her personal life she had formed a serious relationship with someone who considered himself very much an existentialist: W S Merwin, who was a neighbour and friend of the family when Plath lived in Primrose Hill. Plath immersed herself in existentialist thought, both in her reading and in her life. Her poetry, in particular her later work, carries a strong existential influence. Throughout her work she uses what has been described as 'the "recurring themes" of existentialism . . . such themes as freedom, decision, and responsibility; . . . finitude, alienation, guilt, death; . . . intensity.'[32] Existentialism, which stressed the importance of personal experience and responsibility and the demands that they make on the individual who is regarded as a free agent in a deterministic and seemingly meaningless universe, was a theory which Plath related to exceptionally well. Her study of personal relations showed that the assumption of responsibility and an honest engagement with life were what she considered prerequisites for a genuine relationship.

This existential stance came to the fore towards the end of Plath's life. In 'Letter in November', (*CP*, pp. 253–4) the speaker comes alive in the appreciation of the beauty of her garden; this appreciation of beauty, as it presents itself in the moment, is also the theme of 'Getting There' (*CP*, pp. 247–49): 'the black car of Lethe', the eradication of personality which results in a new identity at the end of the poem is strikingly similar to existential theory, and in particular to the theories put forward by Jean-Paul Sartre, who believed that at the heart of a human being was a 'nothingness', out of which 'he' created 'himself'.[33] In 'The Applicant' (*CP*, pp. 221–2) the candidate is shown to be deficient, sadly lacking, and incorporating in a joking manner the 'nothingness at the heart of being' which existential theory propounds.

Plath's existential viewpoint is shown most distinctly in a poem written only ten days before her death; 'Mystic' (*CP*, pp. 268–9) is directly concerned with uncovering some meaning to life. 'The air is a mill of hooks/Questions without answers', to which the speaker finds no respite either in religion ('The pill of the Communion tablet') or passion ('Is there no great love only tenderness?'). She is caught in the quintessential existential dilemma of angst, with no reliability to be found anywhere, with even the natural world defiled by pollution: 'the fetid wombs of black air under pines in summer.' Having experienced intensity and passion – 'Once one has been seized up/Without a part left over' – there is no way back into an unquestioning, unconscious existence. Eileen Aird's criticism of this poem finds that 'various reactions to morality are examined but rejected, and the greatest pain strikes with the reluctant return to the new day with its muted beauty.'[34] This in fact does not do Plath's vision or conclusions justice. In spite of the myriad disappointments and the painful transience of love and experience, there is a realisation to be made which alone makes life worthwhile and immensely pleasurable.[35] The meaning of life is to be found in no big dramatic event, but in an appreciation of life as lived in the present moment:[36]

Meaning leaks from the molecules.
The chimneys of the city breathe, the window
    sweats,
The children leap in their cots.
The sun blooms, it is a geranium.

The heart has not stopped.

The 'heart' is both synonymous with that of the speaker and the universe.[37] The absurdity of life is redeemed by an awareness and appreciation of all its many facets and beauty. This conclusion is one that held good for Plath the humanist throughout her life, and one that made her poems on the question of religious issues so challenging and courageous.

5. The Short Sharp Shock

Such is the preoccupation of critics with Plath's untimely death that an important characteristic of her work has been ignored: humour. Apart from references to the subject in her novel, *The Bell Jar*,[1] the range of humour in the rest of her work, especially her poetry, has largely been overlooked. This distorts the overall critical reception and effect of her *oeuvre*. An understanding of how and for what reason Plath used humour in her poetry shows how expansive and imaginative her perspective was; it also serves to dent her mythical image as a doom-, death-ridden poet.

Plath used humour in her work to make people laugh, to ridicule and satirise people and customs she considered ripe for criticism.[2] Expert in its craftsmanship, Plath's poetry demonstrates her ability to play with language; her work abounds in puns and one-liners which serve to reinforce their content. There are strong influences of the work of the quirky cartoonist Charles Addams, and mock-Gothic scenarios which thread through several of her poems. Her work also reveals cinematic influences, ranging from German Expressionist films to the *film noir* and gangster movies, so popular in North America in the 1950s. And contradicting several critics who have claimed that Plath took herself too seriously and was guilty of a narcissistic self-obsession, her work reveals numerous instances of self-irony.

Plath's use of humour is not only pleasurable for its own sake, it also has the capacity to reveal hidden and important depths in the content of her poetry. Just as she sought to achieve a healthy balance in her life,[3] so in her poetry the use of humour provided an important counterweight to the serious news of the issues she was dealing with.

Making people laugh

Making people laugh is an aim that Plath had from early on in her career.[4] In a letter to her mother dated 16 April 1955, she described a reading of her poems, entered in the Mount Holyoke College poetry competition:

> The reading went excellently, and I loved doing my poems, because they all sounded pretty polished and the audience was immensely responsive, laughed in some of the witty places even, which made me feel tremendously happy. I think I'd love being a humorous public speaker. It's such fun to be able to make people laugh.[5]

And in an interview given in 1958 she commented on how important it was to her make her poetry humorous: 'I like the idea of managing to get wit in with the idea of seriousness, and contrasts, ironies.'[6]

Her comments in a BBC radio broadcast in September 1962 on Americans living in Britain underscored her aim to be witty. A guest staying overnight at an English home, she was offered the choice of 'hot water bottle or cat. She [the hostess] didn't have enough hot water bottles to go round or enough cats to go round. But if she used both of them they came about even. And I chose the cat.'[7]

Playfulness with language

At the beginning of her career Plath wrote with a thesaurus beside her, experimenting with verse forms and a wide range of words and phrases. Part of her experimentation was to be found in her delight at playing

70

around with language, creating bites of sound in the mode of Gerald Manley Hopkins and Dylan Thomas, two of her heroes.[8] Plath was aware that entertaining her readers through a playful use of language would also help to offset and underscore the serious message and tone underlying much of her poetry.

Several critics have pointed out Plath's playfulness with language.[9] This technique is particularly obvious in her early poems, such as 'Alicante Lullaby' written in 1956 (*CP*, p.43), where the humour springs from the hyperbolic collection of sound effects, as in the last stanza:

> O Cacophony, goddess of jazz and of quarrels,
> Crack-throated mistress of bagpipes and cymbals,
> Let be your *con brios*, your *cappriccios*
> *rescendos, cadenzas, prestos* and *prestissimos*,
> My head on the pillow
> (*Piano, pianissimo*)
> Lullayed by susurrous lyres and viols.

In 'The Ghost's Leavetaking' (*CP*, pp. 90–1) Plath plays around with the theme of ghosts, jocularity showing through the lines:

> The oracular ghost who dwindles on pin-legs
> To a knot of laundry, with a classic bunch of sheets
>
> Upraised, as a hand, emblematic of farewell.

While in 'Heavy Women' (*CP* p. 158) the juxtaposition of two unlikely similes undermines the pomposity of the mothers-to-be:

> Irrefutable, beautifully smug
> As Venus . . .
>
> Smiling to themselves, they meditate
> Devoutly as the Dutch bulb

And in 'Face Lift' (*CP* pp. 155–6) the cosmetic surgery victim wheels off under her own sedated haze to the operating theatre: 'Fizzy with sedatives and unusually humorous,/I roll to an anteroom . . .'

Plath's playfulness with language serves not only to counterbalance critical opinion of her as morbid and death-obsessed but also demonstrates her immense versatility and craftsmanship. Her control of language is very apparent.

Gentle amusement

Plath's use of humour for gentle amusement motivates many of her poems about children and giving birth. It shows the range of her subject-matter as much as her technical ability. *The Bed Book*, published posthumously in 1976 is a humorous rhyming catalogue of beds, full of enjoyable nonsense-verse, as shown by the following two stanzas:

In an Elephant Bed
You go where you please.
You pick bananas out of the trees.

If the tigers jump up
When you happen to sneeze
Why, they can't jump higher
Than the elephant's knees.

The poem 'Metaphors' (*CP*, p. 116), written in 1959 is a game poem which sets out a puzzle in its first line: 'I'm a riddle in nine syllables'. It then proceeds to overflow with exaggerated and unconventional metaphors for pregnancy: 'An elephant, a ponderous house,/A melon strolling on two tendrils.' The woman carries within her 'a red fruit, ivory, fine timbers', by reference to the two preceding lines the most valuable and integral feature within her. The metaphors culminate in the final lines that seem to give the lie to the uncomplicated mirth earlier in the poem: 'I've eaten a bag of green apples,/Boarded the train there's no getting off.'

The ecstasy of being pregnant is deflated through the unpleasant reality of morning sickness and the loss of power embodied in embarking on a journey the outcome of which cannot be terminated.

Ridicule and exaggeration

Plath had a keen awareness of social issues and social behaviour, as her *Journals* and her mother's book *Letters Home* testify. She had an equal loathing for pretentiousness and affected gentility. This dislike is shown throughout her poetry through her use of ridicule and hyperbole to deflate what she considered ripe targets. The poems in which these techniques occur are not straightforwardly humorous however as they are motivated by a strong sense of injustice.

In 'Gigolo' (*CP*, pp. 267–8) the speaker is someone whose narcissism knows no bounds and who therefore becomes quite ridiculous:

> The tattle of my
> Gold joints, my way of turning
> Bitches to ripples of silver
> Rolls out a carpet, a hush.
>
> . . . I
> glitter like Fontainebleau.

Barbara Hardy has commented that in this poem 'the flip style has a modishness just right for the caricature of man and of society.'[10]

The sow in the poem of the same name ('Sow', *CP*,

pp. 60–1) becomes a monster, in the best traditions of cartoon culture:

> A monument
> Prodigious in gluttonies as that hog whose want
> Made lean Lent
>
> Of kitchen slops and, stomaching no constraint,
> Proceeded to swill
> The seven troughed seas and every earthquaking
> continent.

But there is a serious vein to this poem. Plath is attacking the greed of the farmer who has won awards for the sow he has made into a disfigured caricature. It lies, in a sorry state with 'Fat-rutted eyes/Dream-filmed . . .'

Wordgames and puns

A keen reader of Salinger's *Catcher in the Rye* and fan of the poets Stevie Smith and E E Cummings, Plath took care to spice her own work with wordgames and puns.

Plath's wordgames have been widely recognized. In 'The Swarm' (1962, *CP*, pp. 215–7), for instance, she comes up with a line 'Elba, Elba, bleb on the sea', which deflates the pomposity of the Napoleon figure she had been alluding to earlier. Her poetry is replete with puns, some of them not at all explicit, as in the case of the early poem 'Virgin in a Tree' (1958, *CP*, pp. 81–2). Plath uses puns here to sustain a complex effect, simultaneously serious and comic, of different levels of meaning. The poem is about the wasting of youth through spinsterdom, and is presented in a way that is comic but with serious overtones. The girl in question is mocked for her adherence to virginity,

but the poem warns of a bitter future for her. '. . .
Here's the parody of that moral mousetrap/Set in
the proverbs stitched on samplers/Approving chased
[chaste] girls who get them to a tree'; while the later
poetry is replete with more risqué and overtly sexual
puns, as in 'Daddy' (1962; *CP*, pp. 222–4):

> I made a model of you,
> A man in black with a Meinkampf look
> And a love of the rack and the screw.

In 'Fever 103°' (1962; *CP*, pp. 231–2) the sexual
allusions are even more explicit:

> All by myself I am a huge camellia
> Glowing and coming and going, flush on flush.

Plath's recording of this poem, in a stylised, husky
voice, served to simultaneously underscore the overt
eroticism and to satirise it.[11] In 'Lesbos' (*CP*, pp.
227–30) the sexual allusions are highly ironic: 'In New
York, in Hollywood, the men said: "Through?/Gee
baby, you are rare".'

The puns in Plath's poetry were very much part
and parcel of the conversational idiom which marked
her later poetry, and they provided a useful technique
of dealing with what could be regarded as macabre
subject-matter. As P R King has commented, in
'Daddy' the 'light-verse form avoids a lapse into
sentimentality on the one hand and a too strident
personal justification on the other'.[12]

Irony

Marjorie Perloff has commented on how a major
poetic mode found in Plath's poetry prior to 1960
was that of 'ironic understatement, the third-person

poem that sets up an Audenesque contrast between two ways of looking at the same phenomenon.'[13] The third person, who sees more clearly and provides a more realistic assessment of the situation than the subject of the poems, is a prevalent phenomenon in Plath's work. W H Auden is an influence behind the mannered irony of Plath's early work, detected in the distanced, cool voice of the narrator in 'Two Views of a Cadaver Room' (*CP*, p. 114), who sees the lovers' fate more clearly than they do:

> Both of them deaf to the fiddle in the hands
> Of the death's-head shadowing their song.

Emily Dickinson too, with her emphasis on boring beneath the surface situation to reveal the darker side of life and of love, is an influence on the poem 'Spinster' (*CP*, pp. 48–9), in which the woman retreats into the life of a recluse. The irony in the poem is double-edged: not only is the spinster's withdrawal from 'normal' life under attack, but the behaviour of her male suitor is also criticised:

> . . . round her house she set
> Such a barricade of barb and check
> Against mutinous weather
> As no mere insurgent man could hope to break
> With curse, fist, threat
> Or love, either.

In 'Magi' (*CP*, p. 148) Plath focuses on the symbols of good and evil, viewed ironically in their abstractness:

> . . . They're
> The real thing, all right: the Good, the True –
>
> Salutary and pure as boiled water,
> Loveless as the multiplication table.

For the child '. . . the heavy notion of Evil/Attending her cot is less than a belly ache'. The figures of the infant and the abstract figures of religion are juxtaposed in a way which exposes the artificiality and irrelevance behind the religious figure-heads; out of touch with the world of the child, Plath points out with some irony that 'Their whiteness bears no relation to laundry'.

Irony remains a technical device Plath uses in her later poetry,[14] though it functions much more as part of an overall strategy rather than the controlling tone of the poem. In the poem 'Lyonesse' (*CP*, pp. 233–4) the inhabitants of the city sink with it beneath the sea with the remark: 'The Lyonians had always thought/Heaven would be something else'. In 'Daddy' (*CP*, pp. 222–4) Plath creates a line of incomparable irony, which has been taken up by feminist critics: 'Every woman adores a Fascist'. Plath employs heavy irony as the controlling tone of what was apparently the last poem she wrote, 'Edge' (*CP*, pp. 272–3), in the way she depicts the 'achievement' of the dead woman who has also killed her children.

> The woman is perfected.
> Her dead
>
> Body wears the smile of accomplishment,
> The illusion of a Greek necessity
>
> Flows in the scrolls of her toga

Contrary to the view of Plath's work presented by some critics, namely that it is no more than a narcissistic dirge, a number of her poems give evidence of a gentle self-irony. In 'Nick and the Candlestick' (*CP*, pp. 240–2), the speaker declares:

I have hung our cave with roses
With soft rugs –

The last of Victoriana.

She casts a humorous eye both at her attempts to
civilise her surroundings and the incongruousness of
the outfittings. While in 'Letter in November' (*CP*,
pp. 253–4) the speaker paces her garden like an old
colonial, proudly declaring 'This is my property'. As
she walks in her garden she sniffs the plants and
foliage and gently mocks her behaviour, which is
like that of an American tourist: '. . . the wall of
old corpses. I love them. I love them like history.'

Alicia Ostriker has said that in reading the poem 'Cut'
(*CP*, pp. 235–6) 'one feels the weird sinking hilarity
which is an immediate response to any accident'.[15] The
detachment of Plath's speaker is justifiable:

What a thrill –
My thumb instead of an onion.
The top quite gone
Except for a sort of a hinge

Of skin,
A flap like a hat,
Dead white.

It is a detachment which originates from the feelings
of hysteria caused at the outset of any accident. The
poem exploits this feeling through the words which
are over-the-top and a surfeit of historical allusions,
with the cut thumb compared to the pilgrims attacked
by native Americans, the cascade of blood to an
onslaught by the Redcoats in the American War of
Independence, and the elastoplast round the cut to a
'Gauze Ku Klux Klan/Babushka'.

Deflation

Much of the humour in Plath's work is used very clearly to deflate ceremony or behaviour she finds questionable. 'The Times Are Tidy' (*CP*, p. 107) provides a political satire, couched in an idiom based on irony:

> There's no career in the venture
> Of riding against the lizard,
> Himself withered these latter-days
> To leaf-size from lack of action:
> History's beaten the hazard.
>
> The last crone got burnt up
> More than eight decades back
> With the love-hot herb, the talking cat,
> But the children are better for it,
> The cow milks cream an inch thick.

The poem focuses on the collapse of moral standards and the all-pervasive addiction to comfort and conformity which so strongly characterised the 1950s.

The sarcasm employed in 'Wintering' (*CP*, pp. 218–9) is for quite a different purpose. The survivor, 'The woman, still at her knitting,/At the cradle of Spanish walnut,/Her body a bulb in the cold and too dumb to think' is described in Rembrandtian terms with its sharp images of shade and light, but with an aggressive irony which is designed to call the descriptive terms into question. The expression is self-reflective; thinking that the woman is too dumb to think is an assumption of such smugness and unreality that it turns automatically against those who would see her in those terms.

Much of Plath's humour is directed at bringing pompous individuals or figure-heads down to size, as in the poem 'Daddy' (*CP*, pp. 222–4), where the patriarch is 'Not God but a swastika/So black no sky

79

could squeak through'. In the poem 'On Deck' (*CP*, pp. 142–3) the morally righteous evangelist is seen for what she really is:

> The untidy lady revivalist
> For whom the good Lord provides (He gave
> Her a pocketbook, a pearl hatpin
> And seven winter coats last August)

Her mission is to '. . . save/The art students in West Berlin', yet it is clear from her code of values that she has no viable credentials to save anyone.

In 'The Tour' (*CP*, pp. 237–8) a maiden aunt has to come face to face with reality as she tours the premises of her unkempt niece and is confronted with her own pomposity. Her niece mocks her expectations, as she stands in the hall '. . . in slippers and housedress with no lipstick!'; and shows her the anarchic state of her household. At the end of the poem the aunt is unceremoniously sent packing to get her own tea: 'Toddle on home to tea!'

Commenting on both 'Kindness' (*CP*, pp. 269–70) and 'The Tour', Barbara Hardy said:

> Through wildness, caricature and speed these poems attack woman as the conventional keeper of convention. At almost every point in the poetry, the woman's tradition becomes a metonymy for the consumer society – its possessiveness, it materialism, its competitions. The collision between the older conservative women and a younger rebel no doubt has biographical roots.[16]

Standard notions of ghosts and the spirit world in 'The Ghost's Leavetaking' are turned upside-down (*CP*, pp. 90–91), and there are some very spurious presents in 'The Couriers' (*CP*, p. 247). In this poem the speaker urges the person she addresses not to accept the offerings of the couriers:

> The word of a snail on the plate of a leaf?
> It is not mine. Do not accept it.
>
> Acetic acid in a sealed tin?
> Do not accept it. It is not genuine.

The gifts offered are hardly something anyone would be likely to accept; in this complex poem Plath is highlighting the difficulty of recognising what illusion is and what is genuine and worth having. The appalling taste of the lady in the attic is criticised in the poem 'Leaving Early' (*CP*, pp. 145–6), the environment a '. . . jungle of winebottle lamps,/Velvet pillows the colour of blood pudding/And the white china flying fish from Italy.'

In her later poems especially Plath made a concentrated attempt to subvert traditions she found life-denying or constricting. In 'Lesbos' (*CP*, pp. 227–230) and in 'A Birthday Present' (*CP*, pp. 206–8), Plath subverts the housewifely existence and routine; in 'Whitsun' (*CP*, pp. 153–4) the tradition of taking a regimented day out at the seaside comes in for scrutiny; and in 'Face Lift' (*CP*, pp. 155–6) cosmetic surgery is one of the levels of the poem under review.

Satire

A sharp observer of her times, Plath satirises contemporary cinema in a number of her poems. In 'Lady Lazarus', for example, she caricatures the myth of the dumb redhead, who, when she reveals that she is adept at dying, declares: 'I guess you could say I've a call.' But she will have the last laugh; at the end of the poem she declares:

Out of the ash
I rise with my red hair
And I eat men like air.

The dumb redhead, so often satirised in contemporary American cinema (the films of Judy Halliday being a typical example) takes her revenge.

The melodramatic mode, very prevalent in 1950s cinema, is satirised in 'Daddy', with the slow extravagant buildup to the nailing down of the vampire; in the words of 'Lady Lazarus': 'Yes, yes, Herr Professor, it is I'; and the repetition of a threat by the woman in 'Purdah' (*CP*, pp. 242–4,):

I shall unloose
One feather, like the peacock.

I shall unloose
One note

I shall unloose

I shall unloose –
From the small jewelled
Doll he guards like a heart –

The lioness,
The shriek in the bath,
The cloak of holes.

The tradition of *film noir*, the gangster films which had their origin in French cinema of that time, is suitably satirised in 'Death & Co.' (*CP*, pp. 254–5), with its final line: 'Somebody's done for.' This example of a one-liner is typical of Plath's later poetry, couched in a highly colloquial, slangy idiom. In the best tradition of Dorothy Parker and Tallulah Bankhead, Plath shows herself to be a capable exponent of one-liners: as in 'Lady Lazarus': 'Dying/Is an art, like everything else.'

and 'Poem for a Birthday' (*CP*, pp. 131–7): 'This is the after-hell: I see the light.' (Also a pun.) With these pithy, direct statements Plath knocks all ceremony and over-seriousness on the head.

Two early examples of black humour are 'All the Dead Dears' (*CP*, pp. 70–1) and 'The Lady and the Earthenware Head' (*CP*, pp. 69–70). The scene, however, changes in her later work; in 'Among the Narcissi' (*CP*, p. 190), for instance, a macabre joke is being made:

> And the octogenarian loves the little flocks.
> He is quite blue; the terrible wind tries his
>   breathing.
> The narcissi look up like children, quickly and
>   whitely.

In this poem, the suggestion is that the octogenarian is not a completely blameless victim; the language used intimates that he is quite a pompous individual: '. . . Percy/Nurses the hardship of his stitches, and walks and walks.'

The Mock-Gothic and the Absurd

Plath was influenced in her work by expressionism, and by the work of the cartoonist Charles Addams.[17] In a series of poems Plath produced mock-Gothic scenarios,[18] a world celebrated by women writers since the eighteenth century in which reality gives way to fantasy and the supernatural triumphes over the natural. For instance, in 'The Disquieting Muses' (*CP*, pp. 74–6), there is a bald-headed muse, and in 'The Tour' (*CP*, pp. 237–8), a muse looms out of the disorder 'bald' and 'with no eyes', but is, the niece assures her aunt, 'awfully nice' and 'She can bring the dead to life/With her wiggly fingers and for a very small fee.' This Addams-like environment, friendly in its weirdness, also carries undertones of the poetry of Stevie Smith; it is an eccentric world, and one designed to shock. The humour derives from parody of the horror film genre.

As Sandra Gilbert and Susan Gubar aptly describe in *The Madwoman in the Attic*, the female Gothic, 'dramatizations of imprisonment and escape'[19] grew out of the restrictions of a claustrophobic male-dominated society, where women were second-class citizens. The genre became a major resource to women writers, who expressed their vision of the world in fantasy and oblique imagery. The Gothic opened up to fiction the realm of the irrational and of the perverse impulses and nightmarish terrors that lie beneath the orderly surface of the civilised world. Plath's creation of a mock-Gothic in her poetry is in keeping with her objectives as a writer, which were to protest against inhumanity. Mock-Gothic scenarios served a double purpose: to show that constriction and repression of women would no longer be tolerated (a feminist statement well in advance of the second wave of feminism which came to the fore in the late 1960s), and to deflate the arrogant opposition of those who wanted to maintain the status quo.

Throughout much of her poetry the influence of the Absurd is notable.[20] The Absurd, derived from existentialist philosophy, was based on the idea that the world is neither designed nor predictable but is irrational and meaningless. The playwright Eugene Ionesco, whose work Plath liked, was a leading exponent of this philosophy. His work was remarkable for its mixture of social satire, Alice in Wonderland logic, verbal hysteria and surrealist farce.

In 'Lady Lazarus', for example, there is the woman as circus-performer, carrying out a death-ritual for 'the peanut-crunching crowd'. Like her counterparts in German expressionist films (such as the shadowy figures in

The Cabinet of Dr Caligari and *Nosferatu*, and the robot/false Maria in *Metropolis*) she is an outlandish figure, equally outcast and potentially dangerous, as is the speaker in 'Fever 103°':

> The beads of hot metal fly, and I, love, I
>
> Am a pure acetylene
> Virgin

A Bride of Frankenstein figure. Here the mock-Gothic meets the Absurd, with chillingly hilarious results. The Absurd runs through scenarios such as 'The Applicant', who is required to be alarmingly defective in order to qualify for the product the salesman is selling, and in 'An Appearance' (*CP*, p. 189) where the woman becomes a machine: 'From her lips ampersands and percent signs/Exit like kisses.'

Far from being gloomily obsessed with death, Plath's poetry is rich in many varieties of humour. Plath uses macabre images to poke fun at what she considered to be pretentious and spurious values. She employed humorous devices to satirise and parody customs and people she considered guilty of injustice. Humour in the poetry was very much a tool of protest, but it was also present to entertain, and she had a delight in the playfulness of language. Her creation of a mock-Gothic, in which the claustrophobic restrictive influences on women's lives were depicted only to be systematically deflated and used as parodies, was an element of the tremendous power that informed her poetry. Humour provided a competent balance for the controversial and serious subject-matter she dealt with. As her poems show, she could hold her own with any humourist.

6. Standing Outside the Mainstream

Plath's social awareness

In a decade when women were encouraged to forget their wartime forages into independence and to see their goals in life as being good housekeepers, wives and mothers,[1] poetry became a genteel profession, dominated by the discreet Marianne Moore and Elizabeth Bishop. Marianne Moore was famous for her light rhyme, critical essays and reinterpretation of fairy-tales, while Elizabeth Bishop's work recreated idiosyncratic worlds and reflected a female sensibility within the rigorous framework of formal verse. Though their contemporary, Plath was totally opposed to the rigid formality and nebulous quality of their work. She wrote with great fervour against the materialism of the 1950s and upheld the importance of the spiritual welfare of humankind and individual responsibility for the welfare of others. Her commitment to social engagement, which in her work evoked echoes of W H Auden, derived in part from the American tradition of High Idealism, leading back through Waldo Emerson to the first American poet Anne Bradstreet. It was also in keeping with her own family background.[2] Brought up in a middle-European family, with an Austrian mother and Prussian father, Plath had a strong internationalist perspective. Throughout her life, while staunchly American, she fostered a keen interest in her own family background and was always very concerned about the implications of American foreign policy on Europe and the rest of the world.

Her studies at Cambridge University, where she met her future husband Ted Hughes, intensified her political awareness. In 1955 she declared: 'The international outlook is the coming world view, and I hope to be a part of that community with all I have in me.'[3] She became rapidly disenchanted with what she perceived to be an extreme insularity in English social and political life: 'I am so prejudiced against it [England] in . . . politics, class-system, medical system, fawning literary cliques, mean-minded critics.'[4] Plath made it plain that she felt a sense of duty to the world, in keeping with the humanist philosophy she followed:

> . . . I have always wanted to combine my creative urges with a kind of service to the world. I am not a missionary in the narrow sense, but I do believe that I can counteract McCarthy and much adverse opinion about the U.S. by living a life of honesty and love . . . It is, in a way, serving my religion, which is that of humanism, and a belief in the potential of each man to learn and love and grow: these children, their underdeveloped lands, their malnutrition – all these factors are not the neat rigid American ideals, but I believe the new races are going to influence the world in turn, much as America did in her day, and, however small my part, I want a share in giving to them.[5]

Plath's horrified reaction to the execution of the Rosenbergs, judged guilty of espionage (an incident which featured in *The Bell Jar*) revealed the strength of her pacifist convictions:

> They were going to kill people with those atomic secrets. It is good for them to die. So that we can have the priority of killing people with those atomic

secrets which are so very jealously and specially and inhumanly ours.

There is no yelling, no horror, no great rebellion. That is the appalling thing. The execution will take place tonight; it is too bad that it could not be televised . . . so much more realistic and beneficial than the run-of-the-mill crime program. Two real people being executed. No matter. The largest emotional reaction over the United States will be a rather large, democratic, infinitely bored and casual and complacent yawn.[6]

The concern Plath showed in her life and her work for the decline in moral standards and what seemed to be an almost irrevocable trend towards dehumanisation was something she shared with her two great role-models Virginia Woolf and D H Lawrence. Throughout his life Lawrence warned against the dangers of an unquestioning worship of technology: 'While the soul really lives, its deepest dread is perhaps the dread of automatism. For automatism in life is a forestalling of the death process', while Woolf, normally so cool and dispassionate in her writing, wrote vehemently against the destructiveness and aridity of patriarchal society.[7] Plath's treatment of the theme of misplaced values is also very much a sign of a feminist stance she adopted from the outset of her career, as Wendy Martin has commented:

Male writers are permitted to articulate their aggression, however violent or hostile; women writers are supposed to pretend that they are never angry. Sylvia Plath refuses to honor this concept of feminine decorum and dares to express her negative emotions . . . Plath chooses to be true to her experience and to her art rather than to the traditional norms of feminine experience.[8]

A rejection of automatism

The poem 'Night Shift' (*CP*, pp. 76–7), written in 1957, is a condemnation, strongly reminiscent of W H Auden, of automatism in the workplace. In this poem the workers in a factory have become so accustomed to the deafening noise of machinery, 'that muted boom' that 'nobody/Startled at it, though the sound/Shook the ground with its pounding'. The factory interior is a nightmarish place resembling the scenario depicted in Fritz Lang's classic film *Metropolis* (1929).

> . . . immense
>
> Hammers hoisted, wheels turning,
> Stalled, let fall their vertical
> Tonnage of metal and wood;
> Stunned the marrow.

Oblivious of the fact that there is nothing life-enhancing in their work – 'It was not a heart, beating' – the

> . . . Men in white
>
> Undershirts circled, tending
> Without stop those greased machines,
> Tending, without stop, the blunt
> Indefatigable fact.

With a perverse tenderness they expend their energy caring for something inhuman which will continue without them and is threatening their existence. The ambiguity of the title 'Night Shift' emphasises the irony of the situation.

Writing on the cumulative psychological damage created by mass production, the sociologist David

Meakin has commented: 'Far from providing integration and fulfilment, such work seems rather to isolate the worker, to demoralize him and replace hope for any other kind of satisfaction by resignation to a sort of ersatz fulfilment in the acquisition of consumer goods. This transference of emphasis from creation to consumption is one of the most characteristic features of our civilization and culture'.[9]

Spiritual deprivation and the death of the psyche provides the theme for several other poems. In 'Whitsun' (*CP*, pp. 153–4) there is no respite from automatism, even on a bank holiday outing. The beach is peopled by a bleak collection of 'Grownups coffined in stockings and jackets,/Lard-pale, sipping the thin/Air like a medicine'. Unable to relax and enjoy themselves they 'idle/As if in hospital'. The picnic takes place 'in the death-stench of a hawthorn', while the only living thing seems to be the sea: 'The waves pulse and pulse like hearts', as the speaker and her partner lie 'Seasick and fever-dry'.

Plath warns of the insidious danger of living in the shadow of the machine. An existential crisis, on which the psychoanalyst Rollo May has commented:

The danger always exists that our technology will serve as a buffer between us and nature, a block between us and the deeper dimensions of our own experience. Tools and techniques might be an *extension* of consciousness, but they can just as easily be a *protection* from consciousness.[10]

Life is reduced to a mechanical process in 'Totem' (*CP*, pp. 264–5): 'The engine is killing the track', while people with 'eyes mica-silver and blank,/Are riding to work in rows, as if recently brainwashed' in 'Insomniac' (*CP*, p. 163). The paralysis of the human psyche through unquestioning adherence to consumerism and unrewarding and unstimulating work was a great danger to be feared. In her *Journals* Plath wondered 'how human beings can suffer their individualities to be mercilessly crushed under a machinelike dictatorship, be it of industry, state or organization, all their lives long'.[11]

Consumerism

Behind the drive for efficiency at all costs lay an emphasis on consumerism. In a society where a feeling of community had been dramatically eroded and material values only were recognised, even human suffering had become merely something to savour and enjoy, just another consumer product.[12]

In 'Aftermath' (*CP*, pp. 113–14) the crowd of onlookers 'Compelled by calamity's magnet' are denied satisfaction: 'Cheated of the pyre and the rack,/The crowd sucks her last tear and turns away.' The same vampire-like people[13] resurface in the later poem 'Lady Lazarus' (*CP*, pp. 244–7) as 'The peanut-crunching crowd' come to see Lady Lazarus's ultimate striptease – her own self-destruction. The insidiousness of the consumer stance shows itself in the sly irony of 'Cut' (*CP*, pp. 235–6), in which the speaker having cut herself reverts to automatic pilot, parading learned behaviour as she treats this experience as something to be thoroughly exploited and enjoyed. Enjoyment is one of the immediate sensations triggered by the shock of realising an accident has taken place:

Your turkey wattle
Carpet rolls

Straight from the heart.
I step on it,

Clutching my bottle
Of pink fizz.

Plath satirises this consumerist attitude towards every
facet of life which she regarded as a knee-jerk reaction
– to the dangerously powerful advertising industry in
the 1950s America which sold everything from household goods to a way of life, and in particular the way
women were supposed to live their lives. (Plath had
been exposed to the glossy world of advertising and
high fashion with the time she spent at *Mademoiselle*
and the experience had left its mark.)

The all-pervasive influence of the advertising industry is characterised very effectively in 'The Applicant'
written in 1962 (*CP*, pp. 221–2). Here, the vocabulary
of the advertising industry resounds. The applicant
needs to be 'our sort of a person', defined as someone
with 'Stitches to show something's missing', 'Rubber
breasts or a rubber crotch', essentially some kind
of freak. This applicant is offered 'A living doll' to
make good his/her deficiency.[14] The 'doll' requested
to 'come out of the closet' is hyped as a panacea for all
the applicant's ills – it is there 'To bring teacups and
roll away headaches/And do whatever you tell it'. In
fact, it is the angel in the house, the Victorian little
woman, who has now become the perfect machine:

It can sew, it can cook,
It can talk, talk, talk.
It works, there is nothing wrong with it.[15]
You have a hole, it's a poultice.
You have an eye, it's an image.

In this persiflage of the advertising industry the most
horrific side-effect is the degradation of women: no
longer individuals in their own right, they exist
only to service terrifyingly deficient partners. This

92

poem contrasts with 'The Tour' (*CP*, pp. 237–8), which radically reverses the adman's dream.[16] Plath cleverly deflates the virtues of 'the little woman' and the perfect household so pervasively promoted by the media at that time. The 'tour' is around a house that is far from being the ideal home; it is in fact an adman's nightmare. The owner 'in slippers' and 'housedress with no lipstick' shows the sights to the maiden aunt who has 'come to call'. The tone is sarcastic and playful as the speaker enjoys disappointing her visitor's expectations; her place is: '. . . a bit burnt out,/A bit of a wild machine,[17] a bit of a mess!'

The machines in this household are indeed anarchic; the washing-machine with its ad name 'Morning Glory Pool' ate 'seven maids and a plumber/And returned them steamed and pressed and stiff as shirts.' As in cartoons by Charles Addams, which appear to have influenced the poem, nothing is actually as it appears: the speaker warns her visitor:

> O I shouldn't put my finger in *that*
> Auntie, it might bite!
> That's my frost box, no cat,
> Though it *looks* like a cat, with its fluffy stuff,
>   pure white.

The furnace 'exploded one night' with 'each coal a hot cross-stitch – a *lovely* light', leaving the speaker bald, like the 'nurse' – synonymous of the muse who also has no eyes, but who is, the speaker assures her visitor, 'awfully nice'. Having confounded and rendered her unwanted prim and proper guest powerless, she who so openly disapproves of her lifestyle, the speaker finally and exultantly sees her off, knowing that she has won a battle in the supremacy pecking order: 'Well I *hope* you've enjoyed it, auntie!/Toddle on home to tea!' The final line with its irony shows auntie's defeat;

there will be no tea for her unless she makes it herself at her own place.

Automatism and the Holocaust

In a number of poems Plath explores the effects of automatism which led to the Holocaust. Here Plath connects with her Prussian/Austrian heritage and modern European tradition, in particular the German poet Paul Celan, who wrote about the horror of the concentration camps and the resulting guilt and shame of the German people.[18] Throughout her life Plath explored her Germanic background, having visited Germany while on her Fulbright scholarship and having intended to go on a trip to Germany and Austria with her brother and sister-in-law in 1963.[19]

Consumerism triumphed obscenely in the Second World War death camps, where parts of human bodies were transformed into commodities by the camp guards. In 'Lady Lazarus' (*CP*, pp. 244–7) the speaker understands how she has become dehumanised and turned into an object merely for her audience's gratification and practical usage:

> . . . my skin
> Bright as a Nazi lampshade,
> My right foot
>
> A paperweight,
> My face a featureless, fine
> Jew linen.

She sees very clearly how she is meant to be a victim, a mere object of the Nazi doctor's appalling experiments:

I am your opus,
I am your valuable,
The pure gold baby

That melts to a shriek.

and how she is meant to lose all mental, emotional and physical identity:

Ash, ash –
You poke and stir.
Flesh, bone, there is nothing there –

Her last lines, warning of revenge, equate the concentration camp doctor with God and Satan, all guilty in her eyes of reducing the human being to a cipher. In this poem Plath argues that the Lady Lazarus figure is the kind of revenging conscience which an oppressive and morally deficient society deserves,[20] as she rises phoenix-like at the end of the poem, red like mother earth, to exact a terrible vengeance. The intensity of her revenge is justified by the equally intense and flagrant abuse of man by man.

The Nazis' success in their mass extermination practices was because of their ruthless efficiency and the perverse use to which they put the latest technological advances. In this context even the most neutral objects take on a sinister function. For example, in several of Plath's poems a train features as an ominous machine which is identified with destruction and sadism: in 'Daddy' (*CP*, pp. 222–4) it is 'An engine, an engine/Chuffing me off like a Jew./A Jew to Dachau, Auschwitz, Belsen'. The starkness of the image intensifies alarmingly in 'Getting There' (*CP*, pp. 247–9). The 'train is steaming./Steaming and breathing, its teeth/Ready to roll, like a devil's.' It is 'dragging itself, it is screaming –':

An animal,
Insane for the destination,
The bloodspot,
The face at the end of the flare.

Plath's war poetry

In the 1950s, with the constant threat of an imminent nuclear holocaust and daily stress of the Cold War, all of which Plath felt acutely and reflected in her work, letters and journals, the world seemed a powder keg of regional conflicts. As the speaker in 'Getting There' exclaims wearily: '. . . it is some war or other.'

Plath's 'war' poetry is in line with the war poems of Wilfred Owen, whose work impelled agreement through the density and accuracy of its imagery, and its skeletal matter-of-fact quality is similar to the verse of the Apocalyptic poets. Her approach, however, is very different. Even poems, which at first sight revolve around war imagery, extend their reference: 'Daddy' is about destructive personal relationships as well as war; while 'Lady Lazarus' and 'Getting There' are about conflict but also rebirth. Each poem can be interpreted in various ways, and the combination of the interpretations provide an overall extremely powerful statement.

Plath was gravely concerned about the destructive capacity of the USA and the USSR, and worried about the fate of her own children and of children throughout the world. After the Russian invasion of Hungary and the Suez crisis, Plath wrote to her mother in a strong pacifist tone:

> . . . no war, after these mad incidents has any meaning for us. All I think of are the mothers and children in Russia, in Egypt and know they don't want men killed . . . I wish Warren [her brother] would be a conscientious objector. It is

96

wrong to kill; the rationalizations of defense and
making peace by killing and maiming for decades
are crazy . . .[21]

The first excursion she took her baby daughter
Frieda on was a demonstration against the H-bomb
in London:

> I found myself weeping to see the tan, dusty
> marchers, knapsacks on their backs – Quakers
> and Catholics, Africans and whites, Algerians and
> French – 40 percent were London housewives. I
> felt proud that the baby's first real adventure
> should be as a protest against the insanity of
> world-annihilation. Already a certain percentage
> of unborn children are doomed by fallout and no
> one knows the cumulative effects of what is already
> poisoning the air and sea.[22]

'Fever 103°' (*CP*, pp. 231–2, the title a metaphor for
the feverish Cold War climate at that time, in addition
to referring to the speaker's illness) focused on the
effects of atomic warfare and radiation. Horrified, the
speaker fears the use of the bomb will lead directly to
the destruction of humanity:

> Such yellow sullen smokes
> Make their own element. They will not rise,
>
> But trundle round the globe
> Choking the aged and the meek,
> The weak
>
> Hothouse baby in its crib,
> The ghastly orchid
> Hanging its hanging garden in the air,

Devilish leopard!
Radiation turned it white
And killed it in an hour.

Greasing the bodies of adulterers
Like Hiroshima ash and eating in.
The sin. The sin.

What especially worried Plath was that not only had war become an unexceptional everyday occurrence, but also that the power to start or prevent new wars lay in the hands of those she considered most morally flawed: business men. It is business men, who make the speaker of 'Fever 103°' see herself as a commodity: 'My head a moon/Of Japanese paper, my gold beaten skin/Infinitely delicate and infinitely expensive.'

Consumerism and politicians

Plath's horror at the 'terrifying mad, omnipotent marriage of big business and the military'[23] was clearly expressed in an article written for the *London Magazine* in 1962, while a year before she had written to her mother of her increasing concern for the future in a world where all moral values seemed to have been cast aside:

> . . . I got so awfully depressed two weeks ago by reading two issues of *The Nation* – 'Juggernaut, the Warfare State' – all about the terrifying marriage of big business and the military in America and the forces of the John Birch Society, etc.; and then another article about the repulsive shelter craze for fallout, all very factual, documented, and true, that I simply couldn't sleep for nights with all the warlike talk in the papers, such as Kennedy saying Khrushchev would have 'no place to hide', and the

armed forces manuals indoctrinating soldiers about the 'inevitable' war with our 'implacable foe' . . . I began to wonder if there was any point in trying to bring up children in such a mad, self-destructive world.[24]

Human life lay precariously with 'the terrible/brains of Krupp', the architect of the German war effort in the Second World War ('Getting There'),[25] with the 'man with grey hands' who 'smiles/The smile of business, intensely practical' ('The Swarm', *CP*, pp. 215–17).

Plath recognised that everything was capable of being reduced to the mechanics of a business deal, and death was no exception, as the poem 'Death & Co.' (*CP*, pp. 254–5) exemplifies,[26] where the two faces of death try to cajole and persuade the speaker into entering into a contract with them, which would end in death.

The only way Plath saw to resist the negative and life-denying influence of the business world was to directly challenge its values and beliefs, which is what she did in 'The Tour' and even more forcefully in 'Stings' (*CP*, pp. 214–15) in which the queen bee – a personification of the speaker –

> . . . is flying
> More terrible than she ever was, red
> Scar in the sky, red comet
> Over the engine that killed her –
> The mausoleum, the wax house.

As well as being one of her favourite symbols, the bees have a particularly relevant significance. As Carole Ferrier has indicated, in ancient times the bees symbolised a well-ordered society, but in modern times they stand for the indiscriminate masses.[27]

Plath did not hesitate to criticise what she found

wrong. She was highly aware of the insidious threat McCarthyism posed to everything she believed America should stand for. As she wrote to her college friend and confidant Ed Cohen:

> You're a Communist nowadays if you sign peace appeals. Ed, people don't seem to see that this negative anti-Communist attitude is destroying all the freedom of thought we've ever had . . . Everything they don't agree with is Communist.[28]

A staunch Democrat, Plath warned her mother against voting for Nixon in the 1960 presidential election: 'His record is atrocious from his California campaign on – a Machiavelli of the worst order.'[29] She had earlier been incensed at the Tories' invasion of Suez.[30]

In her poems of social protest, Plath identified herself with what have subsequently been regarded as feminist aims and objectives, as defined by Plath's contemporary and rival Adrienne Rich:

> Feminism means finally that we renounce our obedience to the fathers and recognize that the world they have described is not the whole world. Masculine ideologies are the creation of masculine subjectivity; they are neither objective, nor value-free, nor inclusively 'human'. Feminism implies that we recognize fully the inadequacy for us, the distortion, of male-created ideologies, and that we proceed to think, and act, out of that recognition.[31]

Caring for the environment

Caring for an environment under threat from the abuse of technology is the theme of several of

Plath's poems and it is a theme which connects her with Wordsworth and the Romantic poets and with D H Lawrence. With their criticism of conventional morals, the dehumanisation of life and their focus on the genuine, essential self, both Lawrence and Woolf voiced concerns at the very heart of Plath's work.

The environment and the sea were important elements in Plath's emotional landscape. She grew up in the small coastal town of Winthrop, Massachusetts. As she recalls in a BBC broadcast in 1962: 'My childhood landscape was not land but the end of the land – the cold, salt, running hills of the Atlantic. I sometimes think my vision of the sea is the clearest thing I own'.[32] Her disillusioned return to Winthrop Bay many years later as an adult, to its spoiled 'tawdry harbor', its 'drabbled scum' to 'a churlish welcome' is charted in the poem 'Green Rock, Winthrop Bay' (*CP*, pp. 104–5).

In 1956, shocked and horrified by the invasion of Hungary by the USSR and the escalation of the Cold War, Plath wrote to her mother: 'The creative forces of nature are the only forces which give me any peace now.'[33] With the breakup of her marriage in 1962, Plath's instinctive reaction was to go to Ireland to find peace and relaxation in an unspoiled environment. 'I will try to rent the house for the winter and go to Ireland – this is a dream of mine – to purge myself of this awful experience by the wild beauty I found there.'[34] In an earlier letter she had described her aspirations as a writer: 'my songs will be of fertility of the earth.'[35] Plath's belief that humanity had to live in harmony with the natural environment, coupled with her very real horror of man's flagrant abuse of nature, remained constant leitmotifs throughout her work.

In the poem 'Blue Moles' (*CP*, pp. 126–7) the speaker envies the easy, unthinking, existence of the animals observed:

. . . still the heaven
Of final surfeit is just as far
From the door as ever. What happens between us
Happens in darkness, vanishes
Easy and often as each breath.

'Medallion', with its echoes of Lawrence's 'Snake',[36] focuses on the beauty of the snake which has been destroyed by indiscriminate violence: 'Knife-like, he was chaste enough,/Pure, death's-metal. The yardman's/Flung brick perfected his laugh.' The cruelty and wanton destruction of nature is also the subject of 'Pheasant' (*CP*, p. 191). Here the attitudes of the speaker and the speaker's partner contrast sharply. While the partner wants to kill it, the speaker values the pheasant's beauty: 'It's such a good shape, so vivid./It's a little cornucopia,/It unclaps, brown as a leaf, and loud'. The speaker recognises the human intrusion as the pheasant:

Settles in the elm, and is easy.
It was sunning in the narcissi.
I trespass stupidly. Let be, let be.

The last line is an ominous indication that efforts to keep it from being killed will not prevail.

The destruction of nature is also the theme of 'Private Ground' (1959; *CP*, pp. 130–1). The speaker in this poem seems almost hermetically sealed off from the world around her in a synthetic, poisonous world:

A superhighway seals me off.
Trading their poisons, the north and south bound cars
Flatten the doped snakes to ribbons. In here, the
    grasses
Unload their griefs on my shoes.

Plath's nature poems warned of the cumulative end result of pollution and disregard for the natural environment. In 1962 Plath wrote that she was concerned about 'the incalculable genetic effects of fallout.'[37] This theme runs through a number of poems. It provides the subtext for 'Fever 103°' and is also the underlying current through 'Thalidomide' (*CP*, p. 252), the sphere of reference of which extends beyond the contemporary drug scandal.[38]

In 'A Birthday Present' (*CP*, pp. 206–8), a poem centred on release as a 'birthday present' from a constricting lifestyle, the bleak, claustrophobic environment of the speaker is threatened by 'clouds' that are 'armies' of 'carbon monoxide'. They fill her: '. . . veins with invisibles, with the million/Probable motes that tick the years off my life.' The horror of contamination also runs through 'Mary's Song' (*CP*, p. 257), where there is no longer any security or safety. The speaker in this poem sees the corpses of the Jews turning into 'thick palls' that:

. . . float

Over the cicatrix of Poland, burnt-out
Germany.
They do not die.

Technology is destructive: from its use in preparing animals for human fodder – 'The Sunday lamb [with its connotations of Christ] cracks in its fat' – to its use in the wholescale mass-murder of concentration camp victims, it has become all-pervasive. Life in the age of technology has become a nightmare. It is no longer safe to take anything at face value. The speaker needs to reassure herself that 'It is a heart,/This holocaust I walk in'.

The poem 'Contusion' (*CP*, p. 271) drives home the lethal nature of this type of pollution. Here, the human body, like the world, has become frighteningly vulnerable, to the extent that even a bruise can become fatal:

> The size of a fly,
> The doom mark
> Crawls down the wall.
>
> The heart shuts,
> The sea slides back,
> The mirrors are sheeted.

Not only has the misuse of technology damaged the environment, it has also backfired on those who are responsible and it now threatens human life.

Nature untamed

With the poem 'Watercolour of Grantchester Meadows' (*CP*, pp. 111–12), written in 1959, Plath attacks another facet of 'automatic living', the attempt to place artificial bounds on nature. The poem rejects the suburban park, the 'country on a nursery plate' with its 'meadows of benign/Arcadian green', the embodiment of a 'genteel' nature. The 'Spotted cows revolve their jaws and crop'. Everything is ominously well-ordered: 'The blood-berried hawthorn hides its spines, with white,' and the people too have become just another ordered piece in this jigsaw: '. . . the students stroll or sit,/Hands laced, in a moony indolence of love.' The speaker longs for the wildness of an untamed environment, in which 'The owl shall stoop from his turret, the rat cry out'.

'Sleep in the Mojave Desert' (*CP*, pp. 143–4), a poem Plath described as 'a coloured postcard from the wilderness',[39] centres on just such an environment. Here it is 'dry, dry/And the air dangerous'. The connection with the 'civilised' world is tenuous in the extreme, with a line of poplars 'the only/Object beside the mad, straight road/One can remember men and houses by'. The desert, though a hostile, unaccommodating environment, is nevertheless alive, teeming with a myriad animals, fighting it out: 'Snake and bird/Doze behind the old masks of fury', 'the lizards airing their tongues/In the crevice of an extremely small shadow/And the toad guarding his heart's droplet' while the speaker and companion are also both assimilated in the same struggle to survive: 'We swelter like firedogs in the wind.'

In this context it is interesting to note that the poems Plath wrote about the landscape of Yorkshire and its moors, an equally inimical environment, are unreservedly uniformly bleak and negative. In 'Wuthering Heights' (*CP*, pp. 167–8), for instance, the setting is nightmarish: 'The grass is beating its head distractedly./It is too delicate/For a life in such company;/Darkness terrifies it.' Ironically, Plath wrote a sombre poem 'November Graveyard' (1956, *CP*, p. 56) on the very place she ended up being buried in. This is a cold skeletal environment where there is: '. . . rot/To unpick the heart, pare bone/Free of the fictive vein.' Here 'Flies watch no resurrection in the sun'. Plath's poems on this environment are replete with references to the people who inhabit this landscape, for the most part sombre and unflattering: in 'Wuthering Heights' the landscape is held blameless for its bleakness; rather, the blame is attributed to the mean-mindedness of the inhabitants: '. . . in valleys narrow/And black as purses, the house lights /Gleam like small change.'

'Two Campers in Cloud Country' (*CP*, pp. 144–5) focuses on the regenerative aspects of living in peace with, and respect for, the natural environment, an environment that is both untamed and unthreatening. This poem, culled from a cross-country trip Plath made with her husband across New England into Canada in the summer of 1959, is strongly reminiscent of Keats. Looking for 'a vacation/Where trees and clouds and animals pay no notice;/Away from the labelled elms, the tame tea-roses', where 'It is comfortable, for a change, to mean so little', the speaker finds herself in a country outside of the rules of suburban life: 'In this country there is neither measure nor balance.' Out in this wilderness human life pales into insignificance, completely overshadowed by the natural environment as 'The pines blot our voices up in their lightest sighs.' But this is a positive transformation, healing and relieving the old worries and concerns:

Around our tent the old simplicities sough
Sleepily as Lethe, trying to get in.
We'll wake blank-brained as water in the dawn.

The restorative capacity of nature is at the heart of a number of poems, particularly the later ones. In 'Among the Narcissi', written in 1962 (*CP*, p. 190), the flowers are 'vivid as bandages' and the man is 'mending' in their presence. The beauty of flowers gives unexpected pleasure, relieving an otherwise grey existence, in 'Poppies in October' (*CP*, p. 240). They are:

A gift, a love gift
Utterly unasked for
By a sky

Palely and flamily
Igniting its carbon monoxides, by eyes
Dulled to a halt under bowlers.

They are the one living thing in the traumatised world around the speaker, whose life-force seems drained by the impersonal and destructive automatism controlling life around her; and the one thing which revives her awareness of her own life: 'O my God, what am I/That these late mouths should cry open/In a forest of frost, in a dawn of cornflowers.' Similarly, in the poem 'Tulips' (*CP*, pp. 160–2) the vitality of the flowers as they open up and move in the sunlight in her hospital room are sufficient to inspire the speaker to regain her life.

These poems, in which nature is charged with a significance beyond its physical qualities, show the influence of the Romantics on Plath's work, in particular that of Wordsworth, Blake and Shelley. In 'Letter in November' (1962, *CP*, pp. 253–4), for instance, it is the speaker's garden that is holding out against the 'thick gray death-soup', which is at once both the impending winter and also, by implication, the polluted environment. Because of the beauty of her garden and the life within it, the world 'Suddenly turns, turns color' as she inspects her 'property', childlike in her exuberance: 'My wellingtons,/Squelching and squelching through the beautiful red.' But the poem ends on an ominous note. The 'Seventy trees/Holding their gold-ruddy balls' are likened to 'the mouths of Thermopylae', as 'The irreplaceable/Golds bleed and deepen'. Heroically, as in the historical parallel, where a small, largely outnumbered force of Spartans held out against the Persians in their invasion of Greece, the trees, and by extension the speaker and nature itself, are ultimately doomed as they are up against odds that will in time overcome them. As Plath warned in her verse drama 'Three Women' (*CP*, pp. 176–87) the abuse of the environment has become a 'time bomb' and the earth will have its revenge: 'Men have used her meanly. She will eat them./Eat them, eat them, eat them in the end.'

In her concern for the environment Plath set the pace for women poets who followed her. As Alicia Ostriker has commented, they are now 'delicately but firmly reversing the assumption of man's division from nature.'[40]

Plath had a strong social awareness, which she expressed throughout her poetry, highlighting issues which were not only of immediate concern but which have remained relevant up to the present time. Like Woolf and Lawrence before her, she rejected automatism, which she saw as an insidious threat to life. She was equally concerned about the seemingly irreversible trend towards an all-pervasive consumerist society. Plath's war poetry demonstrated her belief that the role of a poet was to be a spokesperson. She had a keen sense of moral injustice and was extremely wary of politicians and the power which they wielded in conjunction with big business. A 'green' poet long before the ideas inherent in the notion of 'greenness' became acceptable, let alone fashionable, Plath demonstrated the overriding need to integrate humanity within the environment and other living things and to stop pillaging and polluting the earth's resources.

Plath's was clearly no anthropocentric vision, but rather that of someone who valued and respected life in all its forms. She was prepared to fight against what she regarded as immoral and destructive forces.

7. The Plath Technique

Plath had a fresh and innovative approach to conventional subject-matter, such as relationships and religion. She had a creative style which evolved to become one of the most distinctive in contemporary poetry, and certainly one which never fails to leave an impact.

Ted Hughes has commented on her instinct to make order out of chaos:

> She was fond of drawing . . . preferably something complicated and chaotic, like a high heap of junk. On her paper this became inexorably ordered and powerful . . . [it] took on the look of her poems, everything clinging together like a family of living cells, where nothing can be alien or dead or abitrary.[1]

Her poetry was tightly structured, centred around a system which gave her work the appearance of an organic whole, with every image, every idea, echoing another, a multifaceted kaleidoscope. That this was her intention is made clear in a radio broadcast she gave in 1961:

> A poem can't take the place of a plum or an apple. But just as painting can recreate, by illusion, the dimension it loses by being confined to canvas, so a poem, by its own system of illusions, can set up a rich and apparently living world within its particular limits.[2]

Plath's early technique

Plath's style underwent a radical development, contemporaneous with the change of direction in the content of her work. She had started out in the words of Robert Lowell, who had her in his writing class at Boston University as:

> . . . a brilliant tense presence embarrassed by restraint. Her humility and willingness to accept what was admired seemed at times to give her an air of maddening docility that hid her unfashionable impatience and boldness. She showed us poems that later, more or less unchanged, went into her first book, *The Colossus*. They were somber, formidably expert in stanza structure and had a flair for alliteration and Massachusetts low-tide color.[3]

In an interview given in 1958 Plath commented on how this low-key style, expertly structured, was what she was after:

> Technically I like it to be extremely musical and lyrical, with a singing sound. I don't like poetry that just throws itself away in prose. I think there should be a kind of constriction and tension which is never artificial yet keeps in the meaning in a kind of music, too. And again, I like the idea of managing to get wit in with the idea of seriousness, and contrasts, ironies, and I like visual images, and I like just good mouthfuls of sound which have meaning . . . At first I started in strict forms – it's the easiest way for a beginner to get music ready-made, but I think that now I like to work in forms that are strict but their strictness isn't uncomfortable. I lean very strongly toward forms that are, I suppose, quite

rigid in comparison certainly to free verse. I'm much happier when I know that all my sounds are echoing in different ways throughout the poem.[4]

Two years later she was to dismiss everything she had written prior to 'The Stones' the seventh and last section of 'Poem for a Birthday', as juvenilia,[5] and to say that the poems Lowell had seen bored her since they were not written to be read out.[6]

Plath's technique evolved along with her development as a writer; some technical devices remained constant, reinforcing the view of her work as a complex tapestry, while others were discarded over time as she found a way through to her own idiom and thematic landscapes.

In an introduction to a broadcast of her poems, made in 1961, she said:

> They are, quite emphatically, about the 'things of the world'. When I say 'this world' I include, of course, such feelings as fear and despair and barrenness, as well as domestic love and delight in nature. These darker emotions may well put on the masks of quite unworldly things – such as ghosts, or trolls, or antique gods.[7]

Greek myths

Ancient gods provided the basis for Plath's original poetic technique and provided an erudite flavour to her work, in keeping with the genteel modernism of the decade. The early poems abound in references to Greek mythology, which often seem contrived. 'Conversation Among the Ruins' (*CP*, p. 21), written in 1955, has the speaker 'Composed in Grecian tunic and psyche-knot' – a caricature of formality – while 'Winter Landscape, with Rooks' written the same year (*CP*, pp. 21–2) the sun is 'an orange cyclops-eye'. 'Two Sisters of Persephone', written in 1951 (*CP*, pp. 31–2) focuses on the two lives lived by Persephone; in the darkness and aridity of the underworld for half the year and in fertility on the earth for the other half.[8] 'Faun' (*CP*, p. 35), a poem about a return to primitivism and influenced by D H Lawrence, casts the lover in a Dionysian mould.

The allusions to Greek mythology continued to provide what was usually a forced frame of reference throughout 1958, a year when, as Ted Hughes remarks, 'Sylvia Plath found writing difficult', and when 'she resorted to set themes, and deliberate exercises in style, in her efforts to find release'.[9] Poems based loosely and somewhat peripherally on Greek myths abounded during this period: 'Virgin in a Tree' (*CP*, pp. 81–2) and 'Perseus' (*CP*, pp. 82–4) were both commissioned for *Art News*; and it was in 1958 that she also wrote 'In Midas Country' (*CP*, pp. 99–100), while in 1959 three somewhat contrived poems on the Electra theme appeared – 'The Eye-Mote' (*CP*, p. 109), 'Electra on the Azalea Path' (*CP*, pp. 116–17), which she found 'too forced and rhetorical'[10], and the title poem of her first book 'The Colossus' (*CP*, pp. 129–30).

Although Plath's use of Greek mythology was later for the most part discarded when she developed her own distinctive style,[11] there is one interesting aspect of her use of these myths which directly foreshadows her later development. The poem 'Aftermath' (*CP*, pp. 113–14), written in 1959, directly likens the victim of an arson attack to 'Mother Medea', in what at first sight seems to be an unflattering comparison.[12] In this poem Plath neatly reverses the original characterisation of Medea in that she depicts her as a victim of society.

Mother Medea in a green smock
Moves humbly as any housewife through
Her ruined apartments . . .

The woman in this poem is a survivor, surveying the damage done to her house and herself, and it is indicated that she deserves to survive in the face of a community that, far from being supportive, is blatantly hostile and ready to enjoy her pain and predicament: 'Cheated of the pyre and the rack,/The crowd sucks her last tear and turns away.'

This is one of several instances when Plath deliberately reverses the original meaning of historical symbols and provides a startling new version, distinctly feminist, where she locates the source of the character's misfortune in the attitudes of society rather than in her own temperament.

The poem 'Purdah' (*CP*, pp. 242–4) provides another instance. In this poem the 'father of the human race' is not a likeable character, rather a 'green Adam' of whom the female speaker is 'the agonized/Side'.

The elaborate interweaving of Greek allusions in the early poetry greatly diminishes in the later work, when Plath found her real voice and no longer needed to borrow either structure or context. The only poem which at first sight seems an exception is 'Medusa' (*CP*, pp. 224–6), about a mother-daughter relationship, with the only concrete reference to Greek mythology in the title which, in a startling way, is extremely apposite. In this poem Plath shows how horrific a mother's constrictions on a daughter can be; the last lines with their reference to the snake-lined hair of Medusa make this very clear: 'Green as eunuchs, your wishes/Hiss at my sins./Off, off, ecly tentacle!/There is nothing between us.' Just as in the Greek myth an unguarded glimpse of Medusa caused death through paralysis, so too, the poem argues, does an unguarded relationship to one's mother cause an equally fatal paralysis of will and action.

In her later poems, Plath discounted and deflated the heavy weight of classicist influences she had infused into her early work. In 'Edge' (*CP*, pp. 272–3) the dead woman's actions are described as 'the illusion of a Greek necessity'. With this line Plath is simultaneously pointing out the spuriousness of the attempt to portray suicide in an admirable light – as an act of idealism – and at the same time mocking the deadweight of classicism which has, with the name of tradition, dogged her poetry and other poetry of the 1950s. The rigid order, so seemingly adhered to previously, is seen for what it is – false and destructive:

> The moon has nothing to be sad about,
> Staring from her hood of bone.
>
> She is used to this sort of thing.
> Her blacks crackle and drag.[13]

Other myths

A number of Plath's poems took their inspiration from other mythologies, as she read anthropological works, encouraged by her husband who was studying the subject at Cambridge. Early poems show that Plath was familiar with African folklore – the poem 'Spider' (*CP*, pp. 48–9) is a direct reference to Anansi, a famous spider trickster hero of West African and Caribbean folklore. The same figure resurfaces later in 'Totem' (*CP*, pp. 264–5), in which the spider has become even more bleak and nightmarish a figure and is ominously equated with God. 'The Bull of Bendylaw' (*CP*, p. 108) shows Plath's knowledge of Celtic mythology and legend. It drew its inspiration from a once-popular Scottish ballad and was a neat paraphrase of this, exemplifying Plath's ever-increasing belief that men were enslaved by their capacity for destructive sexual relationships. 'Lyonesse' (*CP*, pp. 233–4) refers to Arthurian legend and the mythical kingdom of Sir Tristram in South Western England, believed to have been submerged by the sea.[14]

German mythology was also used by Plath as the basis for a number of poems. The central motivation for 'Lorelei' (*CP*, pp. 94–5) was provided in a session with the 'ouija oracle'[15] Ted and Sylvia used on several occasions. The poem derived its force from 'the German legend of the Rhine Sirens, the sea-childhood symbol, and the death wish involved in the song's beauty. The poem devoured my day, but I feel it is a book poem and am pleased with it.'[16] Based on the German legend in which a siren lured sailors to their deaths on the rocks beneath her, this poem explores the danger-zone of attraction and deception and is one of the more successful using a mythological context.

Magic and ouija boards

Parallel to the use of mythology in her work, ran Plath's use of references to magic and ouija boards, to which she refers in letters to her mother and writes about in her journals.[17]

References to magic occur as symbols throughout her work.[18] This theme provided the impetus for a series of poems covering the years 1956–60: 'Recantation' (*CP*, pp. 41–2), 'Crystal Gazer' (*CP*, pp. 54–6), 'The Everlasting Monday' (*CP*, p. 62), 'Ouija' (*CP*, pp. 77–8), 'Dialogue over a Ouija Board' (*CP*, pp. 276–86) and 'The Hanging Man' (*CP*, pp. 141–2). It also provided a subtle framework for much of the rest of Plath's work.

As Plath had commented, the 'masks of quite unworldly things' served as symbols for 'the darker emotions' which she was still to express in a direct form. 'The Hanging Man' is after the tarot card the Hanged Man, whose significance lies in the way he is depicted. His right leg bent behind his left forms a cross, which indicates self-imposed suffering.[19] This reinforces the other context of the poem, which revolves around electro-shock therapy and its outcome.

Bees as symbols

Another set of symbols providing a subtext to Plath's poetry revolved around a subject her father had been an expert in and one which Plath herself researched and practised: entomology.[20]

'The Beekeeper's Daughter' (*CP*, p. 118) provides a variation on the Electra theme, with its sexual imagery and portents of guilt and doom: 'A fruit that's death to taste: dark flesh, dark parings.' Bee imagery took on a central importance in a cycle of poems written sequentially in late October 1962: 'The Bee Meeting' (*CP*, pp. 211–12), for example, is about what on the surface seems a very routine event: the moving of a swarm of bees from one hive to another. The female speaker/protagonist, however, sees herself to be identified with the old queen with whom the new virgins dream of fighting a duel which they will win. When the swarm is moved, the speaker feels that it is her own death which is portended: 'Whose is that long white box in the grove, what have they accomplished, why am I cold.' The routine event becomes a nightmare.

In 'The Arrival of the Bee Box' (*CP*, pp. 212–13) the bees once again are an ominous force which the speaker nevertheless resolves to set free. The last ambivalent line 'The box is only temporary', endorses another, literal, meaning for the bees, representing the life-force and underscored by the pun: 'be(e)s'. The psychological undertones of the poem then become apparent and the bees denoting emotional life and the core of an identity previously repressed beneath the rule of gentility, become apparent.

This reference is carried over into the following poem 'Stings' (*CP*, pp. 214–15), where the protagonist identifies herself with the old queen, still capable of reassuming power:

Now she is flying
More terrible than she ever was, red
Scar in the sky, red comet
Over the engine that killed her –
The mausoleum, the wax house.

The pack of bees is 'A black intractable mind' in 'The Swarm' (*CP*, pp. 215–17), while in 'Wintering' (*CP*, pp. 217–19) the purely female colony of bees surviving the winter has 'got rid of the men,/The blunt, clumsy stumblers, the boors'.

In these late poems Plath used the bee symbols as a leitmotif for her own purposes: the bees, active and pre-eminent in their own well-ordered society, are role-models for women who in the 1950s were denied power and position and as such were subordinate and passive.

Colours

In the earliest poems Plath wrote she employed her unique and intricate colour scheme. Initially it co-exists alongside other systems, but in the later poems it becomes a dominant feature. Plath's use of colours would seem in part to be derived from her training as an artist and also from her readings of mythology; she had read and been impressed by Fraser's *Golden Bough* and Robert Graves' *The White Goddess*.

The poem 'Apprehensions' (*CP*, p. 195–6) is about the uncertainty of life after death; it is centred around the significance of colours, as the direction of the poem moves from a positive 'green' image to a desolate 'gray', a defiant 'red', an ominous 'black' and finally to an indecisive 'white'.

The colour black is assigned its traditional meaning in Western culture. Black stands for aggression and destructiveness in nature: 'Against both bar and tower the black sea runs' ('Point Shirley', *CP*, pp. 110–11); in men: 'the black man who/Bit my pretty red heart in two' and the 'man in black with a Meinkampf look' ('Daddy', *CP*, pp. 222–4); for death: 'Death opened, like a black tree, blackly' ('Little Fugue', *CP*, pp. 187–9).

White undergoes a dramatic change in connotation. Initially implying positive qualities of, for instance, innocence and goodness in the early poem 'Recantation' (1956, *CP*, pp. 41–2), where the speaker is exhorted to 'do good/With your white hands', it is demoted in 'Moonrise' (1958, *CP*, pp. 98–9) to sterility. White can, however, also mean fertility: 'White: it is a complexion of the mind . . . The white stomach may ripen yet.' In a poem written the same year and centred round a runaway ride on a horse, it stands for power: 'all colors/Spinning to still in his one whiteness.' ('Whiteness I Remember', *CP*, pp. 102–3). But from the following year onwards the colour assumes negative symbolic meanings. For example, in 'Mushrooms' (1959, *CP*, pp. 139–40) white is the colour of deception:

Overnight, very
Whitely, discreetly,
Very quietly

118

Our toes, our noses
Take hold on the loam,
Acquire the air.

and in 'Stings' (1962, *CP*, pp. 214–15) where 'The man in white smiles.' The colour is synonymous with a destructive idealism and aridity in 'Magi' (1960, *CP*, p. 148):

Their whiteness bears no relation to laundry,
Snow, chalk or suchlike. They're
The real thing, all right; the Good, the True –

Salutary and pure as boiled water,

White is synonymous with violence in 'The Moon and the Yew Tree' (1961, *CP*, pp. 172–3), where the moon is described as 'White as a knuckle', and in 'Totem' (1963, *CP*, pp. 264–5) where it stands for butchery: 'White towers of Smithfield ahead'. It is part of the world of nightmare in 'Three Women' (1962, *CP*, pp. 176–87), where one of the female protagonists rebels against 'that flat, flat, flatness from which ideas, destructions,/Bulldozers, guillotines, white chambers of shrieks proceed; . . . The white clouds rearing/Aside were dragging me in four directions; I do not believe in those terrible children/Who injure my sleep with their white eyes, their fingerless hands.' It stands for lack of vitality in 'The Bee Meeting': (*CP*, pp. 211–12) 'I am exhausted, I am exhausted – Pillar of white in a blackout of knives'; while the 'long white box' containing the old queen is ominously similar to a coffin.

The other two most important and frequently used colours in Plath's work are red and green. Green figures prominently throughout. Usually the colour stands for creativity. In 'Snakecharmer' (1957, *CP*, p. 79), for instance, the artist creates a green world: '. . . Out of this green nest/As out of Eden's navel twist the lines/Of snaky generations'; in 'The Eye-Mote' (1959, *CP*, p. 109) horses are '. . . warped on the altering green', and in 'The Hermit at Outermost House'[21] (1959, *CP*, pp. 118–19) the hermit created:

> . . . a certain meaning green.
> He withstood them, that hermit.
> Rock-face, crab-claw verged on green.
>
> Gulls mulled in the greenest light.

Green stands for the life-force[22] in 'Three Women' (*CP*, pp. 176–187): 'The little grasses/Crack through stone, and they are green with life'; while in 'Letter in November', written in the same year, (*CP*, pp. 253–4): 'There is a green in the air,/Soft, delectable./It cushions me lovingly.'

The colour red is most salient in the later poetry. It very often represents vitality. For instance, in 'Apprehensions' (1962, *CP*, pp. 195–6): 'This red wall winces continually:/A red fist, opening and closing,/Two gray, papery bags'; in 'Poppies in October' (1962, *CP*, p. 240) 'Even the sun-clouds this morning cannot manage such skirts,/Nor the woman in the ambulance/Whose red heart blooms through her coat so astoundingly'. Sometimes the colour is the symbol for the earth and Mother Nature, as in 'Berck-Plage' (1962, *CP*, pp. 196–201): 'Six round black hats in the grass and a lozenge of wood,/And a naked mouth, red and awkward'; and in 'Brasilia' (1962, *CP*, pp. 258–9): 'Red earth, motherly blood'. It is the colour of revenge in 'Lady Lazarus' (1962, *CP*, pp. 244–7): 'Out of the ash/I rise with my red hair/And I eat

120

men like air.' And red is the colour which symbolises both creativity and vitality in 'Ariel' (1962, *CP*, pp. 239–40), where the movement is 'Into the red/Eye, the cauldron of morning'.

Other symbols

Plath's later work is characterised by symbols which echo each other and link up in a surrealistic fashion to form a distinct kaleidoscope. The intricate symbolism of the late poems has often posed a stumbling block for critics. She assembles a symbolic tapestry of her own (an arrow, smiles, the moon, the sun, mirror images, horses, trains, a cauldron) and through repetition[23] they become appropriate. She described this innovative and anti-academic stance in a letter to her mother in 1958, in which she also expressed her reserve about teaching:

> . . . the writer is cut off from life and begins to *think* as he analyzes stories in class – very differently from the way a writer *feels* reality, which, according to many teachers, is too simple as such and needs symbols, irony, archetypal images and all that. Well, we will try to get along without such conscious and contrived machinery. We write and wake up with symbols on our pages, but we do not begin with them.[24]

As in the short story 'Smile', written by one of Plath's favourite authors, D H Lawrence, smiles become synonymous with deception and malicious intent. In 'Berck-Plage' (*CP*, pp. 196–201) the female protagonist affects a form of behaviour she thinks will protect her from the danger she senses around her: 'Why is it so quiet, what are they hiding?/I have two legs, and I move smilingly.' The participants of

'The Bee Meeting' (*CP*, pp. 211–12) 'are smiling and taking out veils tacked to ancient hats', taking part in a ritual which has a frighteningly sinister outcome; in 'The Swarm' (1962, *CP*, pp. 215–17) smiles are inextricably associated with ruthlessness and inhumanity: 'The man with grey hands smiles – The smile of a man of business, intensely practical'; the smile is a weapon in 'The Detective' (*CP*, pp. 208–9): '. . . this is a man, look at his smile,/The death weapon' and 'The Other' (*CP*, pp. 201–2): 'You smile./No, it is not fatal'; while it is an automatic gesture of one of the two faces of death in 'Death & Co.' (1962, *CP*, pp. 254–5) and the sign of delusion and perversity in Plath's last published poem 'Edge':

The woman is perfected.
Her dead

Body wears the smile of accomplishment,
The illusion of a Greek necessity[25]

Many of Plath's later poems revolve around a journey. In 'Getting There' (*CP*, pp. 247–9) and 'Lady Lazarus' (*CP*, pp. 244–7) the journey is from a life of abuse and nightmare to one of liberation; likewise in 'Ariel' (*CP*, pp. 239–40) the journey is from a static, death-like existence to an autonomous, positive and active life, as in 'Fever 103°' (*CP*, pp. 231–2).

The most significant symbol used by Plath in her later poetry, is that which deliberately reverses the conventional or expected meaning. Plath uses the arrow, traditionally a phallic symbol, to symbolise female energy and creativity. Her later poetry is distinguished by the use of the first person, with the almost always female speaker being placed in the all-important and powerful role as protagonist in a dramatic situation. In her favourite poem 'Ariel' (*CP*,

pp. 239–40) Plath engineered the dramatic
from stasis to intense activity on a variety
Here the female becomes an active par
her own life, taking on the role and symbolic power
traditionally associated with men: '. . . I/Am the
arrow,/. . . The dew that flies[26]. The female speaker
stops being passive and instead takes control of her
life on every level, thereby becoming powerful and
positive.

Several other protagonists in Plath's later poetry
also take control and win through to a position of
power which they have previously been denied.[27]
Thus in 'Daddy' (*CP*, pp. 222–4) Plath neatly
reverses the situation of the passive female figure
in the nursery rhyme 'The Old Woman who lived in a
shoe'. This time the dominance of the male authority
figure is thrown off:

> You do not do, you do not do
> Any more, black shoe
> In which I have lived like a foot
> For thirty years . . .

Similarly, Plath reverses the standard connotations
of moon (female) and sun (male), both important
symbols in her work.[28] In 'Lesbos' a poem exploding
conventional expectations, the moon is characterised
as male, while the sun appears as a female symbol in
'Ariel'. The moon stands for the Muse in 'The Moon
and the Yew Tree' (*CP*, pp. 172–3), where it battles for
the soul of the speaker with the yew as a standard bearer
for religious faith, and in 'Edge' (*CP*, pp. 272–3); while
the sun is a 'red/Eye' a positive and creative force 'the
cauldron of morning' in 'Ariel' (*CP*, pp. 239–40).

Other symbols which Plath used were the mirror,
which stood for the alter ego, as in the poem of the
same name ('Mirror', *CP*, pp. 173–4) – Plath's thesis

on the double in Dostoevsky is influential here; the horse, a symbol of vitality, a key symbol in poems such as 'Ariel' (*CP*, pp. 239–40) and 'Sheep in Fog' (*CP*, p. 262); trains, as in the above-mentioned poem and 'Getting There' (*CP*, pp. 247–9) and 'Totem' (*CP*, pp. 264–5), where they are symbolic of a technological nightmare. Plath also uses flowers as symbols. For example, poppies, which symbolise life in 'Poppies in July' (*CP*, p. 203) and 'Poppies in October' (*CP*, p. 240), as do the tulips in 'Tulips' (*CP*, pp. 160–62) and the narcissi in 'Among the Narcissi' (*CP*, p. 190). A symbol which occurs frequently in the last poems is blood, another symbol of vitality, as in the poem 'Kindness' (*CP*, pp. 269–70): 'The blood jet is poetry,/There is no stopping it.'

All Plath's symbols provide a leitmotif which interconnect, centred as they are around the focus point of vitality and creativity.

Synaestheticism, cinematic techniques and metaphor

Alongside Plath's innovative symbols, there are three key technical aspects which distinguish a Plath poem: the synaesthetic effect, her use of cinematic techniques, particularly in the later poems, and her remarkable use of metaphor, unparalleled since Blake and Dickinson.

Synaesthesia, the experience of two or more modes of sensation when only one sense is being stimulated, was an apt device Plath employed to extend the frame of reference in her poems. It is prevalent throughout her work, an early example occurring in 'Night Shift' (1957, *CP*, pp. 76–7). In a description of the factory at night '. . . the sound/Shook the ground with its pounding', the preponderance of long vowel sounds evokes the physical sensation of the sound. In the verse play 'Three Women' (*CP*, pp. 176–87), giving birth is vividly described in both its audio and physical form: '. . . I am drummed into use.' The accident victim in 'Poppies in October' (1962, *CP*, p. 240) is viewed from a startling perspective, where she is seen on a parallel with the rest of the natural environment; her '. . . red heart blooms through her coat so astoundingly'. An exploration of a garden in winter conveys the physical sensation of contact: 'My wellingtons/Squelching and squelching through the beautiful red.' ('Letter in November', *CP*, pp. 253–4). While appropriately, in the existential poem 'Mystic' (1963, *CP*, pp. 268–9), the world comes alive on many levels: 'The chimneys of the city breathe, the window sweats.' In 'Edge' (*CP*, pp. 272–3) the garden, and by extension the world, has become a painfully intense environment, but nonetheless beautiful and vibrantly alive, as it 'Stiffens and odors bleed/From the sweet, deep throats of the night flower'.

Plath's use of synaesthesia not only provides images that shock and are stunningly accurate but also reinforces her belief that all life is inextricably interwoven and interdependent.[29]

Another key characteristic of Plath's late poetry was its cinematic quality; she used a number of techniques employed in film. With her artist's eye,[30] Plath depicts dramatic internal and external landscapes which change scene with alarming and sometimes nightmarish speed.[31] A month before she died, in a radio broadcast, Plath talked about the appeal visual poetry held for her:

. . . this *in*-feeling, this identification with light, trees, water, *things*, is another aspect of the new poetry – everything is listening, trembling, sentient. There is no sure objective ground – stillness and motion, near and far, telescope upsettingly, they become one.[32]

A way into understanding her last poems is to see that they operate within a dramatic context in which a whole range of cinematic techniques are employed – flashback, slow motion, leitmotifs, close-ups – to convey the protagonist's experiential viewpoint. Such poems bear an uncanny resemblance to German expressionist films of the years after the First World War and are in the spirit of Hermann Warm, a set designer for the classic expressionist film *The Cabinet of Dr Caligari*, who thought that 'films must be drawings brought to life'.[33]

In 'Insomniac' (1961, *CP*, p. 163) the blurred outline of the day as seen by the insomniac shapes itself in a cinematic routine: '. . . the old, granular movie/Exposes embarrassments'. The poem 'Berck-Plage' (*CP*, pp. 196–201) also owes much to the cinema. In a fusion of impressionist and expressionist style, it progresses from an initial scene on the beach, where the protagonist makes her way through an outing of handicapped people, to the surrealistic burial of a neighbour. Here the language and context are highly evocative of German expressionism and the best traditions of *film noir* and horror films. The funeral procession is described as:

Following the coffin on its flowering cart like a
      beautiful woman,
A crest of breasts, eyelids and lips

Storming the hilltop

while the faces of the children are:

. . . turning, wordless and slow,

Their eyes opening
On a wonderful thing –

At the funeral there are:

Six round black hats in the grass and a lozenge
   of wood,
And a naked mouth, red and awkward.

For a minute the sky pours into the hole like
   plasma.
There is no hope, it is given up.

In 'Getting There' (*CP*, pp. 247–9) a war landscape
centred on a train journey with scenes of battle
and the implied terminus in a concentration camp
is cleverly set against scenes of an internal personal
conflict experienced by the protagonist, each aspect
carefully juxtaposed and powerfully built up to the
conclusion, reminiscent in its hypnotic intensity of a
Bergman film.[34]

The train is dragging itself, it is screaming –
An animal
Insane for the destination,
The blood spot,
The face at the end of the flare.
I shall bury the wounded like pupas,
I shall count and bury the dead.
Let their souls writhe in a dew,
Incense in my track.
The carriages rock, they are cradles.
And I, stepping from this skin
Of old bandages, boredoms, old faces

Step to you from the black car of Lethe,
Pure as a baby.

Plath's poem 'Daddy' (*CP*, pp. 222–4) has a similar cinematic reference, with parody in the best traditions of Dracula and Frankenstein, couched in a world of innocence and nursery-rhyme language. Internal and external conflicts are once more counterbalanced. At the conclusion of the poem, with the ritual stake in the heart of the vampire, the landscapes fuse and the conflict is resolved, a resolution which strongly resembles Jung's representation of the archetype in its ritualistic form:

> There's a stake in your fat black heart
> And the villagers never liked you.
> They are dancing and stamping on you.
> They always knew it was you.
> Daddy, daddy, you bastard, I'm through.

At Smith College, discussing the use of metaphor in the work of Henry James, Plath declared her intention of creating her own.[35] Her work is redolent with unusual and even shocking examples of metaphor which reveal an uncanny appropriateness.[36]

Two poems on pregnancy, 'Metaphors' (*CP*, p. 116) and 'You're' (*CP*, p. 141) show Plath's capacity for metaphoric effusiveness. And her later poetry abounds in metaphors which show the startling vulnerability of the human body: in 'Elm' (*CP*, pp. 192–3), for instance, the female speaker is: 'Scorched to the root/My red filaments burn and stand, a hand of wires', an appropriate description of the nervy, exhausted state of mind of the protagonist; while in 'Cut' (*CP*, pp. 235–6) the speaker distances herself from the experience and the pain of her cut thumb:

> Little pilgrim,
> The Indian's axed your scalp.
> Your turkey wattle
> Carpet rolls

In a neat reversal the world of nature is imbued with human characteristics: in 'Tulips', (*CP*, pp. 160–2) the flowers 'breathe/Lightly, through their white swaddlings, like an awful baby./Their redness talks to my wound, it corresponds.'; while in 'Poppies in July' (*CP*, p. 203) they are 'A mouth just bloodied' and in 'Poppies in October' (*CP*, p. 240) 'late mouths' that 'cry open'.

There is an interconnection between every element of life that makes these initially shocking images justifiable: 'The world is blood-hot and personal' ('Totem', *CP*, pp. 264–5), while in the existential poem 'Mystic' (*CP*, pp. 268–9) every aspect of the environment is equally valid and beautiful:

Meaning leaks from the molecules.
The chimneys of the city breathe, the window sweats,
The children leap in their cots.
The sun blooms, it is a geranium.

The heart has not stopped.

Plath's ubiquitous use of metaphor served to underline the connection she saw between all forms of life and movement and provided a stylistic harmonisation between the philosophies which influenced her work: romanticism, humanism and existentialism.

Plath also used metaphor to make what can be construed as feminist statements, as, for example, in the revenge of the woman in purdah who emancipates herself ('Purdah', *CP*, pp. 242–4). The poem ends with two lines enhanced by the surrealistic force of the metaphors: 'The shriek in the bath,/The cloak of holes.': There is also the liberated heroine of 'Ariel' (*CP*, pp. 239–40) who declares:

. . . I
Am the arrow,

The dew that flies
Suicidal, at one with the drive
Into the red

Eye, the cauldron of morning.

Plath's use of metaphor is empowering; more direct and ruthlessly consistent than Emily Dickinson, she made language into a verbal assault, exploding any sense of false decorum and repeatedly showing the connections between private and public life.

Plath's unique voice

Plath was a superb technician – the *Collected Poems* testify to her competence in a whole range of verse form and styles, which included sonnets (lyric poems written in one stanza, consisting of 14 iambic pentameter lines linked by an intricate rhyme scheme), for example, 'Sonnet: To Eva' (*CP*, pp. 304–5), sestinas (an elaborate verse form of Italian origin, unrhymed, consisting of six stanzas of six lines each and a concluding tercet), as in 'Yadwigha, On a Red Couch, Among Lilies' (*CP*, pp. 85–6) and villanelles (consisting of five tercets and a quatrain, all based on two rhymes and with later repetitions of lines 1 and 3 of the first tercet), an example of which is 'To Eva Descending the Stair', (*CP*, p. 303).

Ironically, though, this over-emphasis on style served to constrict her voice, as she wrote in a letter to her mother in 1958:

My main difficulty has been overcoming a clever, too brittle and glossy feminine tone, and I am gradually getting to speak 'straight out' and of real experience, not just in metaphorical conceits.[37]

The language of the Confessional poets, such as Robert Lowell, Theodore Roethke, John Berryman and Anne Sexton, clearly influenced her writing, with their use of 'ordinary speech, whether in blank verse, rhymed or no',[38] especially Anne Sexton's work: 'She has none of my clenches, and an ease of phrase and an honesty.'[39] With their exploration of taboo areas of experience and the flaunting of traditional poetry in their use of free verse, they inspired Plath. The 'ease of phrase' she had admired in Sexton's work became evident in Plath's later poems and made a difference to Plath's development as writer. Ornate and wordy, *The Colossus*, her first book, had been extremely elaborate, with the content very nearly subordinate to the style. *Ariel* was to provide a powerful contrast with its impertinent directness, one-liners and electrifying immediacy. Plath commented in an interview given in October 1962:

These ones that I have just read, the ones that are very recent, I've got to say them, I speak them to myself, and I think that this in my own writing development is quite a new thing with me, and whatever lucidity they may have comes from the fact that I say them to myself, I say them aloud.[40]

The voice that speaks in Plath's late poems is reminiscent of J D Salinger and Joyce Cary in its confrontational colloquial tone. These were writers Plath had modelled herself after in her novel-writing.[41] It is a voice which took on the vocabulary of the admen in 'The Applicant' (*CP*, pp. 221–2) and which mocks its audience in 'Lady Lazarus' (*CP*, pp. 244–7):

Dying
Is an art, like everything else.
I do it exceptionally well.

I do it so it feels like hell.
I do it so it feels real.
I guess you could say I've a call.

Plath used colloquial language to break through institutionalised hypocrisy and expose the actual, 'true' state of affairs.

Plath's distinctive voice derives from a sensitive ear and eye applied with care and precision and a studious apprenticeship in verse, encompassing even the more obscure verse forms. Eclectic in her poetic tools, Plath made use of existing mythologies and added her own which provided a leitmotif through her work. Her startling and accomplished use of synaesthesia, cinematic techniques and at times shocking metaphors make reading her poetry an experience which appeals to all the senses, and mark her poetry as extremely distinctive.

The unparalleled directness of imagery and language, especially prevalent in her later work, and balanced by an appropriate modulated tone and rhythm, are what characterise the Plath technique and make it instantly recognisable as well as enjoyable.

8. Coming Into Her Own

Plath developed a unique style and very distinctive philosophy. Using her technique and writing about her concerns, she acquired a universal appeal. Her work is very readily accessible, one of the hallmarks of a great writer, and her immensely powerful, original voice sears through her poems, making a remarkable stylistic, emotional and rational impact.

The dilemma Plath faced throughout her life was one faced by all contemporary women writers; as Alicia Ostriker put it, 'to be a creative woman in a gender-polarised culture is to be a divided self'.[1] Plath's struggle to stay true to her vocation as a writer while at the same time attempting to live up to the ideal of the efficient, all-round woman, wife and mother, is what she expressed in her work as well as in *Letters Home* and her journals.

Identity as a writer

As the following *Journal* entry, dated 1952, shows, she was very much aware of the restrictions placed on how her life should be:

> . . . when asked what role I will plan to fill, I say, 'What do you mean *role*? I plan not to step into a part on marrying – but to go on living as an intelligent mature human being, growing and learning as I always have. No shift, no radical change in life habits.' *Never* will there be a circle, signifying me and my operations, confined solely to home, other womenfolk, and community service, enclosed in the larger worldly circle of my mate, who brings home from his periphery of contact with

the world the tales only of vicarious experience to me, like so: ◎ No, rather there will be two overlapping circles, with a certain strong riveted center of common ground, but *both* with separate arcs jutting out in the world. A balanced tension, adaptable to circumstances, in which there is an elasticity of pull, tension, yet firm unity. Two stars, polarized: ○○ like so. In moments of communication that is complete, almost, like so ◐ almost fusing into one. But fusion is an undesirable impossibility – and quite nondurable. So there will be no illusion of that.[2]

In 1957, having made the decision to abandon the teaching career her mentors had thought so right for her, Plath affirmed her new image of herself: 'I feel terribly vulnerable and "not-myself" when I'm not writing'.[3] But it took years of struggle with the constrictions of the time and with her feelings about herself for her to accept and welcome her identity as a writer. Having written her first poem at the age of 8, Plath worked doggedly at her writing from then onwards, but she was also painfully aware throughout her adolescence and early adulthood how unfashionable it was for a woman to be a serious writer.

At the age of 14 Plath wrote a poem which a colleague of her English teacher found 'Incredible that one so young could have experienced anything so devastating.'[4] Her response was ambivalent, as her diary entry records:

Today, I bought a group of original poems to Mr Crockett . . . He liked 'I Thought that I Could Not Be Hurt' above the rest and encouraged me greatly by remarking that I had a lyric gift beyond the ordinary.

I was overjoyed and although I am doubtful

about poetry's effect on the little strategy of 'popularity' that I have been slowly building up, I am confident of admiration from Mr. C.![5]

She encapsulated her reasons for writing a poem, in 1948, which ended as follows:

> You ask me why I spend my life writing?
> Do I find entertainment?
> Is it worthwhile?
> Above all, does it pay?
> If not, then is there a reason? . . .
> I write only because
> There is a voice within me
> That will not be still[6]

Plath was worried that her writing would automatically make her unacceptable to her peers and the opposite sex. As she wrote to her mother in 1950:

> If I ever catch a man who can put up with the idea of having a wife who likes to be alone and working artistically now and then, I would like to start thinking about where I'll put the emphasis for the rest of my brief life.[7]

That year she achieved her first commercial success with a short story published in the teenage magazine *Seventeen*, which had also published her first adult poem, 'Ode on a Bitten Plum'.[8] Her ambition to write made her wary of dating boys with the same ambition, for she was to find that her success in print would sooner or later sour the relationship.[9] She became very conscious of the prejudice harboured against 'brainy girls', which she later wrote about in her poetry. By the time she was in her final years at high school, she had learned to hide behind a facade of light-hearted wit and pretended naivety. The insecurity she felt about integrating her ambition to be a writer with her wish to be an 'all-round' person, '. . . the student who not only did well scholastically but was socially acceptable to both sexes, and the service-oriented person who made a contribution to her peer group and the community'[10] remained with her throughout her life.

At Cambridge she wrote to her mother about her need to excel beyond any other comparable woman writer[11] and to cope with every sphere of a woman's existence as then prescribed. But the pressure to conform and to put her partner's life and objectives before her own took over. She saw herself very clearly as a woman writer, but also one who should and would be acceptable to men. By virtue of her incessant need to excel in every part of her life, she fell into the trap so aptly described by Alicia Ostriker:

> . . . the twentieth-century poet continues to live in a society which first of all discourages the possibility of an autonomous female identity by defining womanliness primarily in terms of love – selfless connubial love, ecstatic romantic love, nurturing maternal love.[12]

This was the same trap that women poets since the days of Anne Bradstreet had fallen into, the only escape from which was to become a recluse, like Emily Dickinson, or live in a world of fantasy like the Brontës.

Plath worked to promote her husband's work and felt pleased and relieved that his was the couple's first literary success.[13] But her attempts to remain a 'triple-threat woman' began to founder under the pressures of simultaneously teaching at Smith College, trying to run a home, continuing to be her husband's agent and trying to make headway with her own writing. In 1957 disillusionment set in:

> My ideal of being a good teacher, writing a book on the side, and being an entertaining homemaker, cook and wife is rapidly evaporating. I want to write first, and being kept apart from writing, from giving myself a chance to really devote myself to developing this 'spectacular promise' that the literary editors write me about when they reject my stories, is really very hard.[14]

Having finally abandoned teaching, she was even more determined to make her writing pay. As her early journals and letters show, she had always kept a meticulous chart of how much she earned from her writing, and from now on, as she focused on what she regarded her true occupation, financial success became extremely important. A journal entry from 1958 indicates clearly how essential she thought it to make money out of her work: 'Images of society: the Writer and Poet is excusable only if he is Successful. Makes Money.'[15]

As her confidence in her ability to write grew, so too did her ability to pinpoint her main problem, that she had been writing in a 'glossy feminine tone'.[16] The operative word here is 'feminine'; Plath was beginning to reject the restrictive gender role-models which had been crippling her life and that of so many of her peers, in their efforts to live up to the 1950s ideal of the 'angel in the house'. Shortly afterwards Plath took a part-time secretarial job at Boston Massachusetts General Hospital and avidly read the case histories of the predominantly female mental patients. At this time too she started attending Robert Lowell's writing class, where she met Anne Sexton. The self-effacing Sylvia Plath,[17] as she then seemed to Lowell, was the facade Plath continued to present to the world on her return to England.[18] The creative flow of energy, which was to characterise the best work of her life, did not occur until after she had abandoned hope of fulfilling the traditional role as housewife/mother, and after she had separated from her husband.[19] At that point she wrote to her mother that she had begun to write the best poems of her life:

> Every morning, when my sleeping pill wears off, I am up about five, in my study with coffee, writing like mad – have managed a poem a day before breakfast. All book poems. Terrific stuff, as if domesticity had choked me.[20]

It was at this time that she realised her full potential, and with it finally accepted her identity as a writer: 'I am a writer . . . I am a genius of a writer; I have it in me. I am writing the best poems of my life; they will make my name.'[21]

One of the earliest poems reflecting the division Plath felt so acutely in her own life, the division between being a 'real' woman and a writer is 'Two Sisters of Persephone' (*CP*, pp. 31–2), a poem alluding to the daughter of Zeus and Demeter in Greek mythology who was abducted by Hades and made his wife and queen of the underworld, but allowed to leave it for part of the year. In this poem, written in 1956, the lives of two stereotypes are sharply contrasted: 'Daylong a duet of shade and light/Plays between these.' The one who remains indoors working ends up going '. . . graveyard with flesh laid waste,/Worm-husbanded, yet no woman!', the only physical contact being with worms[22], while the bronzed and natural beauty sunning herself contentedly 'Grass couched in her labor's pride,/ . . . bears a king.' The opposition

138

of the life of the academic/writer and wife/mother is phrased here in what appears very much to be a Lawrentian/Woolfian dichotomy. The reference to Persephone further opens up the poem – the writer is equated with the Persephone banished to the underworld for the winter months, while the 'natural' woman is the Persephone whose return to earth reinstates the earth's fertility.

The same disquieting juxtaposition – presented this time as a game, like Russian roulette – provides the theme for a much later poem, 'In Plaster' (*CP*, pp. 158–60), written in 1960 and culled from Plath's experience of an appendectomy. The two sisters of Persephone have now become 'This new absolutely white person and the old yellow one'[23], a newly created persona set against the old, decaying worn one, but there is a striking difference in attitude between 'In Plaster' and 'Two Sisters of Persephone'. Here it is the 'old, yellow one' that is more valuable – 'I gave her a soul,'; it is also the less conventionally appealing figure who ultimately wins out: '. . . One day I shall manage without her[24]/And she'll perish with emptiness then, and begin to miss me.' The two personas on one level represent the white plaster cast the speaker is encased in and the yellow, worn self lying underneath; on another level they represent on the one hand the superficial or socialised self, which has 'a slave mentality', and also the inner or real self, which 'bloomed out of her as a rose/Blooms out a vase of not very valuable porcelain'. The poem ends with an acceptance on the part of the speaker of herself with all her faults: 'She may be a saint, and I may be ugly and hairy,/But she'll soon find out that doesn't matter a bit.'

The growing acceptance of identity as a writer is also the theme of 'Black Rook in Rainy Weather' (*CP*, pp. 56–7), a poem clearly influenced by Ezra

Pound, W H Auden and Wallace Stevens. In this 1956 poem the muse appears in a 'celestial burning', providing a transformation in what appears to be an otherwise uneventful life, giving 'A brief respite from fear/Of total neutrality . . .'. Waiting for the muse is likened to 'The long wait for the angel,/For that rare, random descent.'

'The Disquieting Muses' (*CP*, pp. 74–6), written in the following year, presents what at first sight appears to be the reverse view of artistic inspiration.[25] This poem paves the way through irony and deflation to an acceptance of artistic talent as something alienating and grotesque but nevertheless redemptive in an otherwise powerless existence.[26] The muses in this poem, inspired by a painting by one of Plath's favourite artists, Giorgio di Chirico,[27] are at worst nightmarish, at best comical, creatures with '. . . heads like darning-eggs' who '. . . nod/And nod and nod at foot and head/And at the left side of my crib.'[28] They stand in direct opposition to the mother's efforts to keep order, as they break the study windows in a hurricane and cause the child to fail miserably in a school performance: she stands '. . . heavy-footed . . ./In the shadow cast by [her] dismal-headed God-mothers.' Nevertheless, the speaker discovers that these weird creatures do have something positive to offer after all: 'I learned, I learned, I learned elsewhere,/From muses unhired by you, dear mother.' This is a rebellious taunt prompted over the gift the disquieting muses have to offer – access to a more colourful, freer world, to 'Flowers and bluebirds that never were/Never, never found anywhere.' The muses remain constant if somewhat ominous companions to the child throughout her adult existence:

Day now, night now, at head, side, feet,
They stand their vigil in gowns of stone,

140

Faces blank as the day I was born,
Their shadows long in the setting sun
That never brightens or goes down.

The same image of the muse – always female in Plath's work – as something freakish and Gothic[29] recurs throughout her later work: as an impassive 'nurse' in 'Barren Woman' (*CP*, p. 157): 'The moon lays a hand on my forehead,/Blank-faced and mum as a nurse', as the moon 'bald and wild' she calls 'my mother' in 'The Moon and the Yew Tree' (*CP*, pp. 172–3), written in October 1961, where the muse provides the only moment of relief and hope in an otherwise overwhelmingly bleak landscape. It resurfaces as a multiple image in 'The Couriers' (*CP*, p. 247), written in November:

. . . the immaculate
Cauldron, talking and crackling

All to itself on the top of each
Of nine black Alps.

with the Alps signifying the nine muses of Greek mythology; and in 'The Tour' (*CP*, pp. 237–8), where it appears as a weirdly likeable Charles Addams-like caricature.[30]

There is one poem in particular which openly celebrates artistic talent; it was written on Plath's thirtieth birthday, 27 October 1962, a date she regarded as especially auspicious. In 'Ariel' (*CP*, pp. 239–40) the 'setting sun' of 'The Disquieting Muses' has become the '. . . red/Eye, the cauldron of morning'. A new beginning for the female speaker in her art has also become fused with a new beginning in her own life – she has at last integrated her identity as a writer with her identity as a woman.[30]

There are a number of poems focusing on the

ccess and power of the artist to transform and
hereby redeem his/her environment. The first,
'Snakecharmer' (*CP*, p. 79), written in 1957, is a
surrealistic portrait of an artist who 'As the gods
began one world, and man another,/ . . . begins a
snaky sphere/With *moon*-eye, mouth-pipe.'[32] The
snakecharmer has absolute control over the world
around him, comparable to the power the female
speaker has momentarily in 'The Disquieting Muses.'
He transforms the world around him until, tiring
of it, he reverses the process and '. . . pipes the
world back to the simple fabric/Of snake-warp,
snake-weft.'

'Sculptor' (*CP*, p. 79) was written in 1958 for
Leonard Baskin, the sculptor-friend of the Hugheses
at Smith.[33] In this poem the sculptor also has the
power of life beyond death. It is to the bronze
dead men that the sculptor through his art '. . .
bequeaths/ . . . life livelier than ours,/A solider
repose than death's.' Here, for the first time, this
leitmotif appears in Plath's poetry.

'The Hermit at Outermost House' (*CP*, pp. 118–19)
shows the hermit/artist[34] in a heroic light, standing his
ground against 'Sky and sea horizon-hinged/Tablets
of blank blue, couldn't/Clapped shut, flatten this man
out.' The hermit, a positive alter-ego of the artist,
creates meaning where there was formerly only chaos
and disorder:

> Hard gods were there, nothing else.
> Still he thumbed out something else.
> Thumbed no stony, horny pot,
>
> But a certain meaning green.

As in 'Snakecharmer' the colour green stands for
the vital force of life and art[35] and again, as in the
'Sculptor', the artist not only has control over his art

142

but also, by extension, over his environment. It is interesting to note that in these three poems, which are focused on power and control, the protagonists are all male (referred to in the third person). Plath still had to find her way to openly proclaiming the power of a female protagonist/artist.

The fusion of life with art, the total acceptance of an identity as a writer, is the main theme running through two of Plath's last poems. In 'Kindness' (*CP*, pp. 269–70), written in February 1963, there is no distinction between the life-force in the speaker/protagonist and the flow of creative energy in art: 'The blood jet is poetry,/There is no stopping it'[36] while in 'Words' (*CP*, p. 270), written on the same day, poems occur after the stroke of 'axes' – as in 'Kindness' writing involves tapping into the very source of life. Like the creations of the sculptor, the poems enter an existence of their own, separate from the life of their creator, the individual writer: they are: 'Words dry and riderless,/The indefatigable hoof-taps.' The horse of 'Ariel' without the rider, the poems transcend mortality.

Writing as identity

Just as Plath learned to accept her own identity with pride[37] as a writer, so her poetry came to reflect this confidence and belief in herself. As Suzanne Juhasz has commented:

> Plath's brief career shows a movement away from a brilliant poetry of surfaces strongly influenced by her male masters to a poetry of engagement and integration between self and world.[38]

At this point in her life, when the barriers between herself and her work had finally been removed,

Plath also got in touch with her own identity as an American. In December 1960 she wrote to her mother:

I hope I can persuade the BBC to accept a program about young American women poets which I am drawing up, now that they seem willing enough to record my odd accent.[39]

And she had been asked to organise, present and take part in an American poetry night to be held in the summer of 1963 at the Royal Court Theatre.[40] Commenting on the power of Plath's final work, Alicia Ostriker sees it lying in 'its fusion of personal voice with rational voice in an Americanism which takes the form of strict – or strident – insistence on immediate factual reality . . . achieved . . . by means of poetic technique, again essentially American, which consists in taking poetic risks.'[41]

A review of Plath's poetry shows that attempts to portray her work as a neurotic dirge fail to account for the range of themes and strong prevailing sense of what is moral and just. The influences on Plath's work were many and varied – she read widely and was eclectic in selecting whatever she found useful for her work. The primitivism in her husband, Ted Hughes's, work, his emphasis on the rituals of creation and destruction and man's kinship with nature, which had attracted her to the work of D H Lawrence, helped liberate her from the post-modernist straitjacket of 1950s poetry. The Romantic poets Keats and Wordsworth were the major influence behind her nature poetry; in her 'war poetry', with its vibrant urgency and on-the-edge quality, the notable influences are Wilfred Owen and Apocalyptic poets such as D J Enright and Peter Porter. Dylan Thomas and Gerald Manley Hopkins were models for the insistent sensuousness of her early verse, while her two role-models D H Lawrence and Virginia Woolf provided the moral tone of her poetry against misplaced values.[42] The Confessional poets, in particular Robert Lowell, Anne Sexton and T Roethke, with their flaunting of taboos, paved the way for the confrontational voice in Plath's later poetry. The poetic reality was something Plath had admired in their work, particularly that of her friend and fellow poet Anne Sexton. One of the first modern poets to deal with specifically women's issues, such as menstruation, abortion and lesbianism, Sexton's was a new and fresh voice in a decade renowned for its formalism and the dissociation of feeling.[43]

Plath's work, however, surpassed Confessional writing. Whatever initial impact such poetry had made on her work, she clearly distanced herself from its effusiveness and self-centredness, as the following comment demonstrates. Introducing a reading of her poetry in October 1962 she stressed that her poetry was neither neurotic nor narcissistic, but about enlargement:

I think my poems immediately come out of the emotional and sensuous experiences I have, but I must say, I cannot sympathize with these cries from the heart that are informed by nothing except a needle or a knife, or whatever it is. I believe that one should be able to control and manipulate experience, even the most terrifying, like madness, being tortured, this sort of experience, and one should be able to manipulate these experiences with an informed and intelligent mind. I think that personal experience is very important, but certainly it shouldn't be a kind of shut-box and mirror-looking, narcissistic experience. I believe it should be *relevant*, and relevant to the larger things, the bigger things such as Hiroshima and Dachau and so on.[44]

Making the connection between the personal and the public is a feminist concern. However, for the most part, feminist critics have not claimed Plath as a positive role-model because of the sensational details of her personal life.[45] Yet interpreting Plath's work from the biographical view of a troubled woman poet does not help the reader to recognise the powerful and universally appealing work she wrote. Criticism of her work has meant writers have been discouraged from acknowledging her influence and that a major and important writer has been marginalised.[46]

The issues which concerned Plath, writing in the 1950s and early 1960s, are universal concerns – as she described them:

> the hurt and wonder of loving; making in all its forms – children, loaves of bread, paintings, buildings; and the conservation of life of all people in all places, the jeopardizing of which no abstract double talk of 'peace' or 'implacable foes' can excuse.[47]

These are issues which critics and writers of the present era now recognise to be valid, but this was not the case at the time Plath was writing. The way she dealt with these issues was innovative. As she commented in the same article:

> . . . unless the up-to-the-minute poem grows out of something closer to the bone than a general, shifting philanthropy and is, indeed, that unicorn-thing – a real poem, it is in danger of being screwed up as rapidly as the news sheet itself.[48]

'Close to the bone' was Plath's achievement in her

later and best work, and in the process she heightened the consciousness of readers able to approach her work in an open way.

In spite of the dearth of primary material,[49] Plath has become what she always knew she would become – a household name. A whole Plath 'industry' has come into being – books, plays, dance-theatre, a film.[50] Plath's poetry is now available on record and cassette; the latest collection features her reading her work in the series Great American Poets.[51] There is no doubt that Plath has become big business and that she has succeeded in her aim to make her work '. . . go surprisingly far – among strangers, around the world, even. Farther than the words of a classroom teacher or the prescriptions of a doctor; . . . farther than a lifetime.'[52]

The flourishing Plath industry clearly shows her popularity and the relevance and universality of her work. Unfortunately it has thrived on a horrific and lurid portrayal of the poet, which, as A Alvarez has said:

> misses altogether her liveliness, her intellectual appetite and harsh wit, her great imaginative resourcefulness and relevance of feeling, her control . . . the pity is not that there is a myth of Sylvia Plath but that the myth is not simply that of an enormously gifted poet whose death came carelessly, by mistake and too soon.[53]

It was in an endeavour to correct this distorted image of her daughter that Aurelia Plath published *Letters Home*, but successive books and articles written about Plath seem to have been more concerned with weaving a mythology around her life, rather than interpreting her work and her relevance to readers today.

147

Since her death Plath has influenced many writers throughout the world. She has been acclaimed by feminist critics and imitated by many aspiring writers, but to date no one has caught the fusion of interests and the electrifying intensity so peculiar to her work, the remarkably appropriate combination of style and content which make it possible to speak of the 'Plath poem'.

Plath's value as a writer is considerable. In her poetry she refused to accept a routine existence and instead strove for the moral and ethical values which mark humanity. She was not afraid to tackle 'difficult' subjects, but did so in a way which sought to enhance an appreciation, and improvement in the quality, of life, and to protect those who were vulnerable. Her poetry is intricate and complex, but never obscure and it is very readily accessible.

The enduring success and greatness of Plath's work lies in its universal appeal and in an innovative, effective presentation. Plath was the first writer in modern times to write about women with a new aggressive confidence and clarity, and the first to integrate this confidence and clarity in a sane, honest and compassionate vision.

9. A Biographical Note

Sylvia Plath was born on 27 October 1932 in Boston Massachusetts, the first child of Otto and Aurelia Schober Plath. Both her parents had strong, academic Germanic backgrounds. Plath's father had been sponsored by his grandparents to become a Lutheran minister, but instead chose to become a professor of entomology, becoming a well-known expert in his field. His early death as a result of diabetes in November 1940 when Sylvia was 8 years old plunged the family into financial difficulties, as his wife was forced to amalgamate her household with her parents' and go out to work to make ends meet. Worries regarding financial matters were to remain with Plath throughout her life.

Sylvia and her brother Warren were given an all-round education. Aurelia encouraged them to read at an early age, read aloud to them and took them to the theatre and concerts.[1] On Sundays the Plath children attended services at the local Unitarian church. Plath was set in the mould of a high achiever from a very young age, she produced her first literary success at the age of $8^{1}/_{2}$, with a poem accepted by the the *Boston Sunday Herald*. At high school she scored a very high IQ of nearly 160.

One of the major influences on Plath during her teenage years was her English teacher, Wilbury Crockett. He set high standards for his students, standards which Plath enjoyed living up to. During this time she seemed to him 'an extremely well-adjusted, vibrant, outgoing and brilliant student, always interested in what she read and always willing to talk about her feelings.'[2] Crockett encouraged his students to read widely and in his class Plath first encountered the writers who were to be important influences, such as Virginia Woolf, D H Lawrence, James Joyce, Emily Dickinson and W B Yeats. She also started corresponding with a German student, which reinforced her internationalist viewpoint as they discussed the atomic bomb, the Korean War and the Peace Movement. She was an outstanding student, winning acclaim for her drawings and having a poem published in the *Christian Science Monitor*.[3] While singlemindedly embarked on the first stage of her brilliant writing career, one of her more endearing qualities was also remarked on at this time: her generosity and thoughtfulness towards others. On one occasion a fellow pupil with a speech impediment broke down during class-time, unable to go on with his presentation. Plath immediately came to his aid by taking up the discussion until he was once more able to participate.[4]

Her final year at high school saw the consolidation of her identity as a writer. She submitted work to several well-known magazines, receiving acceptances from *Seventeen*,[5] (in those days the teenage bible) the *Christian Science Monitor* and the *Boston Globe*, earning a total of $63.50. With her growing success as a writer, her popularity also increased. She kept a list of dates, annotated with her own wry sense of humour: one list was headed 'Boys who asked and were unlucky', while her list of excuses for unwanted dates included 'TB or cancer'.[6]

Growing up in the 1940s and 1950s, Plath was acutely aware of the pressure to conform to the media image of the all-American girl, promoted by the bible of the times, Marynia Farnham and Ferdinand Lundberg's *Modern Woman – the lost sex* (1947). Essentially Freudian, its thesis was that women could only find fulfilment through adopting a passive female role the ultimate goal of which was motherhood. The 1950s saw a remarkable rise in the birth rate which peaked in 1957. In that year American women were producing children at a rate unmatched since before the First World War.[7] Plath was fully aware of the restrictions of the age, and she knew about the disadvantages of being a woman: 'Learning the limitations of a woman's sphere is no fun at all' she complained.[8] Excerpts from her diary at the age of 17 reveal how crippling she found the conventions:

> I am afraid of getting older. I am afraid of getting married. Spare me from cooking three meals a day – spare me from the relentless cage of routine and rote. I want to be free . . .[9]

She rounded off her high school education with a record of straight 'A's, winning the award for the most outstanding student. She then decided to go to Smith College, a decision she knew would radically change the course of her life, and one which would also subject her to constant financial pressure since she had to finance her studies through scholarships and housework in exchange for part of the cost of room and board.

When Plath entered Smith in 1950, it was at that time the largest women's university in the world, frequented by daughters of the most affluent families in the land and an academically highly respected institution. She received three scholarships in her first year, including one given by Olive Higgins Prouty, the well-known author of *Stella Dallas*, a novel dealing with the way social barriers constrain and distort emotion, a subject close to Plath's heart. She wrote a letter of thanks, and Mrs Prouty, whom Plath was later to call her 'literary mother'[10] remained a lifelong friend and patron.

151

At Smith Plath continued her relentless drive for academic success, impressing her lecturers with her application and intelligence, but uneasy with the double standards of behaviour. She had a sense of being an outsider, partly because her goals seemed more expansive than those of her peers and partly because she was not able to compete materially with the affluence of her fellow students. In spite of the pressures, however, she found Smith to be the stimulating environment she needed.

Plath remained very much community-oriented. As she wrote to her mother:

> I am starting next Monday to teach art to a class of kids at the People's Institute, volunteer work . . . Next year I hope for either mental or veterans hospital . . .[11]

At Smith she was very much part of the college scene, taking part in the traditional 'step sings' on the lawn in front of the students' building, working diligently on the college paper and getting the right dates, in an effort to live up to the image of the popular, all-American girl. She heard celebrities from the arts and politics, including Nabokov, Robert Frost, W H Auden, and Senator McCarthy, whom she enthusiastically booed along with her peers.[12] The Democrat presidential candidate Adlai Stevenson gave the commencement address in 1955.[13] There seemed no limit to her possibilities:

> The world is splitting open at my feet, like a ripe, juicy watermelon. If only I can work, work, work to justify all my opportunities.[14]

Plath believed in being completely open to experience. In the words of someone who knew her later at Cambridge she 'felt that a drawing back in the face of any aspect of life was nothing less than horrible, a voluntary courting of deformity'.[15] In her relationships Plath was fascinated by experience. For several years she corresponded with a street-wise Chicago student Ed Cohen, who had written her an enthusiastic fan letter after the publication of her poem in *Seventeen*. The same wish for experience motivated the intense but ambivalent relationship she had with Richard Sassoon, a bohemian Yale student related to Siegfried Sassoon.

In 1952 Plath was one of 20 students selected for a guest editorship at the Madison Ave offices of *Mademoiselle*. It was a heady and intense experience. Plath was assigned the job of guest managing editor, the second most important job on the staff, which was also, as one of her fellow students said, '*the* toughest job on the magazine'.[16] At this time Plath appeared 'filled with a healthy love of mankind and great artistic vitality'.[17] As guest editor, some of her duties included reading manuscripts by Dylan Thomas, Noel Coward and Elizabeth Bowen, and commenting on them. She interviewed and lunched with a number of prominent writers, including Marianne Moore and Richard Wilbur. But, as frenetically as she had immersed herself in the world of fashion, as absolutely she withdrew. On her last night in New York, she threw most of her hard-earned wardrobe piece by piece out of her hotel window, watching the clothes sail out over the rooftops. She rejected the materialistic values she had until then worked so hard to assimilate.

On her return home to Wellesley in June 1953, when she found she had not been accepted into Frank O'Connor's prestigious summer school writing course at Harvard, she fell into a depression, unable to continue working on her honours thesis on Joyce's

Ulysses. Unable to cope, Plath took a quantity of sleeping pills, leaving a note for her mother saying she had gone off for a long walk and would return the following day, then hiding herself in the basement of the family home. Some days later her brother heard her moans, and Plath was taken to hospital and slowly and painfully brought back to life.

Olive Prouty arranged for her to be moved from Massachusetts General to the select McLean's in Belmont, a hospital with an outstanding reputation. Here Plath came under the care of an attractive young psychiatrist, Dr Ruth Beuscher. She was to become both a counsellor and role-model for Plath, remaining a close friend for the rest of Plath's life.[18] Dr Beuscher believed that the key to her recovery lay in making Plath able to accept herself for what she was, since her suicide attempt had been motivated by extreme feelings of inadequacy and inability to live up to other people's expectations. Although Plath responded to Dr Beuscher's trust and openness, nevertheless the feelings of alienation and emotional dependency remained with her, as she wrote to Ed Cohen:

> What I need more than anything right now is, of course, most impossible, someone to love me, to be with me at night, when I wake up in shuddering horror and fear of the cement tunnels heading down to the shock room, to comfort me with an assurance that no psychiatrist can quite manage to convey.[19]

Plath returned to Smith in spring 1954, determined to follow Dr Beuscher's advice and break through the sexual double standards. She was held in awe and thrived on her fame. When her short story 'Sunday at the Mintons' took the first prize in a

Mademoiselle competition, her popularity increased dramatically. Yet she still continued to conform to the ground rules. Her Smith room-mate Nancy Hunter Steiner thought that Plath was overly dependent and strangely unwilling to rebel against the conventionality she was so obviously uneasy with: 'Sylvia could not guess that society would ever change; she seemed to see the taboos and tensions of her background as permanent conditions that could not be substantially altered, and she bore them with surface resignation.'[20]

Plath graduated from Smith as one of only four students attaining *summa cum laude* (the highest grade obtainable) that June. She won several awards: for her honours thesis on the double in Dostoevsky's work, for her poetry, and for being the outstanding English student. Her literary success had also been considerable, but the most important of all her achievements was winning a Fulbright scholarship to Newham College Cambridge, which covered all her expenses, including travel, together with a generous book allowance.

At Cambridge Plath had ample time to socialise. In 1955 men outnumbered women 10 to 1 and Plath, attractive and competitive, was in great demand. She led her usual busy life: contributing to the weekly student newspaper *Varsity*, modelling for a two-page feature on fashions, and acting in the Cambridge University theatre group, very much the embodiment of the all-round all-American woman. She also remained a dramatic presence, unconventional and daring.

She continued to apply herself to her studies, especially fascinated by her English Moralists course, taught by Dorothea Krook: 'The one woman I admire at Cambridge! I should grow amazingly by fighting her logically through Aristotle, Plato, through the

British philosophers, up to D H Lawrence.'[21] For her part, Dr Krook found Plath a fascinating student and often extended her tutorials so they could finish their discussions. In spite of the fact that Plath was adept at accumulating 'A's, Dr Krook did not think she was primarily an academic: 'I felt the things I said, we said, her authors said, mattered to her in an intimate way, answering to intense personal needs, reaching to depths of her spirit to which I had no direct access.'[22]

Plath was coasting along when she met the man she was to fall in love with. At that time Ted Hughes was a relatively unknown Cambridge poet. Plath sought him out at the launch of the *St Botolph's Review*, which published his poetry, and their relationship started in the tempestuous way it was to continue:

. . . he kissed me bang smash on the mouth [omission] . . . and when he kissed my neck I bit him long and hard on the cheek, and when we came out of the room, blood was running down his face [omission] and I screamed in myself, thinking: oh, to give myself crashing, fighting, to you.[23]

The objectives Plath had set herself seemed to have been accomplished:

. . . I told myself, coming over, I must find myself: my man and my career: before coming home. Otherwise – I'll just never come home.[24]

Plath married Ted Hughes on 16 June 1956. Soon after, on their honeymoon in Benidorm, she was to express her first misgivings about what she had proclaimed to her friends and family would be an ideal marriage:

156

Up, angry, in the darkness . . . No sleep, smothering . . . The need to go out. It is very quiet. Perhaps he is asleep. Or dead. How to know how long there is before death . . . We go out . . . All could happen: the willful drowning, the murder, the killing words . . . Going back, there is the growing sickness, the separate sleep, and the sour waking. And all the time the wrongness is growing . . . The world has grown crooked and sour as a lemon overnight.[25]

A perfectionist in every aspect of her life, Plath also wanted her marriage with 'the only man in the world who is my match'[26] to be perfect and was to react with intense pain and disappointment when it failed to live up to her expectations.

Graduating from Cambridge with a 2:1, her second BA degree, with which she was disappointed, despite the fact she had already decided to move away from academia, Plath returned with her husband to the USA in 1957, and to a teaching post at her old university, Smith. She proved herself a competent and conscientious teacher, well-liked, teaching students about the writers who had inspired her. Her students admired and were in awe of her. But Plath soon found that teaching was not an ideal way to make a living. The endless corrections and preparation exhausted her, coming on top of the routine household chores and her own attempts to write. After coming down with pneumonia, she decided not to return to Smith for a second year. Determined to continue writing, Plath made plans for them to move to Boston, where they lived until 1959 in a small, cramped apartment on Boston's fashionable Beacon Hill, supplementing their savings by occasional earnings from readings. Plath took on a part-time job at Massachusetts General, transcribing the dreams of patients and acting as receptionist and general office clerk. By December Plath had left her job and was again in the depths of a depression. She immediately began to see her old therapist Dr Beuscher. The rapport and trust she felt with her released her trapped creativity and within a week of starting therapy Plath was again able to write. The therapy helped her to come to terms with the way she viewed her parents and her own relentless perfectionism.[27]

Around this time Plath started to consciously cultivate friendships with women: 'How odd,' she wrote in a journal entry, 'men don't interest me at all now, only women and womentalk.'[28] She also expressed a new aim, to be a writer who was 'a woman famous among women.'[29] She hoped she would be part of a community of powerful women:

I felt mystically that if I read Woolf, read Lawrence (. . . their vision, so different, is so like mine) I can be itched and kindled to a great work: burgeoning, fat with the texture and substance of life: This my call, my work. This gives my being a name, a meaning – 'to make of the moment something permanent:' I, in my sphere, taking my place beside Dr Beuscher and Doris Krook in theirs – neither psychologist, priestess nor philosopher-teacher but a blending of rich vocations in my own worded world. A book dedicated to each of them.[30]

In Boston Plath and Hughes were surrounded by the best the literary world could offer. Plath met Adrienne Rich, whom she considered her greatest living rival, 'who will soon be eclipsed'.[31] She joined Robert Lowell's poetry workshop at Boston University on Tuesday afternoons, where she met Anne Sexton, another poet and a glamorous housewife, who was to become one of her closest friends.

Plath shared her sense of humour and gaiety. After Lowell's classes, accompanied by fellow poet George Starbuck, they would pile into Sexton's old Ford and drive off to the Ritz. Sexton would park in the loading area, telling anyone who challenged them that it was okay since they were only going to get loaded.[32] Lowell gave an account of Plath at that time as 'unusually sensitive and intelligent' and he described her work as 'controlled and modest'.[33]

Plath became pregnant during a cross-country trip in the summer of 1959 and, since they wanted their first child to be born in England, they returned to the UK. Plath hoped that she could have a house help so she would not be submerged by housework. They settled in a tiny flat on Primrose Hill and in 1960 Plath signed a contract with Heinemann for publication of *The Colossus*, her first collection of poetry. Her first child, Frieda Rebecca was born in April of that year, and she was proud and exhilarated to be a mother.

In 1961 Plath had a miscarriage. Shortly afterwards, Alfred Knopf bought the rights to *The Colossus* for publication in the USA, and Plath began to receive major acclaim in her home country. She began to work in earnest on *The Bell Jar*. In late summer of that year the Hugheses moved to Devon, to live in a manor house. Plath, with her usual thoroughness, threw herself wholeheartedly into village life, keeping bees, making jam, attending Sunday service in the local Anglican church and taking an active part in the life of the community; in spite of this, she remained an outsider with few friends in a close-knit community. Aware of her intense need to succeed, Plath was careful to strive for a healthy balance between life and work:

Perhaps the hardest thing I have to accept in my life is 'not being perfect' in any way but only striving

159

in several directions for expression: in living (with people and in the world), and writing, both of which activities paradoxically limit and enrich each other.[34]

In January 1962 Plath's second child Nicholas was born and she began to feel the strain of looking after a large house with two small children, with Ted frequently away in London on business. She continued to seek out women friends. In May 1962 David and Assia Wevill visited. A strong attraction developed between Ted and Assia, who told Plath that her marriage to Hughes was 'little more than a loving friendship'.[35] During Plath's mother's visit that June, things came to a head, to the extent that Plath gathered up the manuscript of her second novel, which focused on her romance and marriage,[36] and burned it in the garden. Aurelia left shortly after, never to see her daughter again. Trying to regain control of her life, Plath again plunged into activity. With the local doctor's wife, she took up riding twice a week, on a horse named Ariel, over Dartmoor, eventually teaching herself to ride bareback. May 1962 saw the publication of *The Colossus* in the USA, as well as several poems in *The Observer*, *Harpers*, *London Magazine*, *Poetry*, *The New Yorker*, *Encounter* and *The New Statesman*. For the first time she was beginning to throw all her energy into making a name for herself as a writer, instead of continually putting her husband's fame first, for whom she had previously willingly acted as agent and secretary.[37] She wrote several book reviews, including reviews of children books,[38] essays for *Punch* and the BBC, finished her radio play 'Three Women' (*CP*, pp. 176–87) and continued to earn as much as she could to get by.

The rift between herself and her husband grew, and in August she wrote to her mother, saying that she intended to get a divorce. A few days later she had a car accident, when her station wagon mysteriously came off the road at high speed; miraculously, she was unhurt.[39] Plath turned in despair to Dr Beuscher, who wrote to her to say that she should rely on her love and support. She advised Plath to take control of her life and get a divorce.[40]

The ideal marriage she had pinned all her hopes on was now falling to pieces. Unable to sleep, Plath rose early and started to write the poems which would make her name. As she wrote to her mother: 'I have it in me. I am writing the best poems of my life; they will make my name.'[41] She worked extensively on the draft of her third novel, *Double Exposure*, which disappeared after her death. In October 1962 Ted moved out for good and Plath made plans to build a new life for herself and the children in London. By mid-November she had selected her 'Ariel' poems for publication. Increasingly, she found encouragement and support from her women friends in Devon and the USA, and she worked to expand this circle. She invited the poet Stevie Smith, whose work she admired, to tea.[42] She also grew closer to her lifelong friend and benefactor Olive Prouty; however, this strong affinity with women, so prevalent in her work, remains largely unrecorded, owing to the lack of biographical material covering the last part of Plath's life.

Plath was fortunate to be able to rent the house in Fitzroy Road, Primrose Hill, where one of her heroes, the poet Yeats, had lived. It was round the corner from where she had previously lived. She took this to be a good omen:

I must be one of the most creative people in the world. I *must* keep a live-in girl so I can get myself back to the live, lively, always learning and developing person I was! I want to study, learn history, politics, languages, travel. I want to be the most loving and fascinating mother in the world . . . I am *glad* this happened and happened *now*. I shall be a rich, active woman . . .[43]

As at each moment of crisis in her life, Plath's answer was to launch herself with absolute intensity into the task of living. But this time the doors of London society were closed. Most of the people she had previously met were also friends of Ted, and conflicts of loyalty arose. Plath struggled on, tired with the task of looking after her flat and her two small children, lonely, hurt and worried with financial matters.

In January 1963 reviews of *The Bell Jar*, which had been published under the pseudonym Victoria Lucas, appeared, for the most part favourable, yet Plath was disappointed because reviewers chose to ignore the main point of the novel – Esther's recovery and reaffirmation of life.

London was experiencing the worst winter it had seen for over 150 years. The heating and plumbing in her house broke down and Plath and the children suffered from recurring colds and 'flu. Without a telephone, which she was waiting to have installed, Plath was completely isolated. Her stamina was low and she was quite clearly affected by the medication her doctor had prescribed.[44] Tragically, just as she was about to achieve literary fame in her own right, the strain of hanging on 'against hard odds and alone'[45] finally told.

Early on the morning of 11 February 1963, after a sleepless night, Plath left food and drink for the children and carefully sealed the door to their room. She then took a large quantity of sleeping pills, switched on the gas, then lay down beside the oven in her kitchen; she had left a note asking for her doctor to be called, his telephone number clearly and carefully written out. The nurse who was employed to look after Plath and the children was delayed in her arrival. When she did arrive and, with the help of workmen, got into the flat, Plath was still warm. She was, however, pronounced dead on arrival at hospital. No will was found, so Ted Hughes took control of her work and became her editor. It is a tribute to the power and brilliance of Plath that, in spite of all the odds she did indeed attain the fame she wanted so badly.

Notes

Chapter 1.

1 For example, 'Sylvia Plath' by the Heidelberg Stadttheater, choreographed by Johann Kresnik in 1985; the Dutch jazz musician Mathilde Santing has set Plath's 'Sheep in Fog' to music; several theoretical pieces have been written on Plath and her work, including 'A Difficult Borning', a collage of Plath's works performed at the New York Studio Theatre in the 1980s by the New York Tea Party, and 'Letters Home' by Rose Leiman Goldenberg, performed in London in 1983; 'The Bell Jar', a film based on Plath's novel, was produced in 1977, and Sandra Lahire produced 'Lady Lazarus', a short film funded by the British Film Institute in 1991. Plath's influence on other writers is worldwide, ranging from the science fiction writer Ursula le Guin to the Chinese poet Duo Duo, testimony to her universal appeal.

2 Ronald Hayman, *The Death and Life of Sylvia Plath*, 1991.

3 Jacqueline Rose, *The Haunting of Sylvia Plath*, 1991.

4 One of Sylvia Plath's closest friends in Devon, Elizabeth Sigmund, has commented on this: 'I have had to endure reading and hearing descriptions of Sylvia and her life which are unrecognisable. To die once is bad enough, but to be repeatedly crucified in this way by people who never knew her is unforgivable. Amateur psychologists have analysed her poetry, people who have never met her have pontificated on her depressive, schizophrenic personality that could not form relationships.' 'Sylvia in Devon: 1962', in *Sylvia Plath: The Woman and Her Work*, edited by Edward Butscher, 1977, p. 107.

5 A Alvarez, *The Savage God: A Study of Suicide*, 1971.

6 Ibid, p. 53.

7   Edward Butscher, *Sylvia Plath: Method and Madness*, 1976, p. 8.
8   Ibid, p. 362.
9   David Holbrook, *Sylvia Plath: Poetry and Existence*, 1976, p. 5.
10 'In Sylvia Plath her false maleness, the animus on which she had to base her identity, comes into conflict with the obvious fact (which she knows from her body) that she was a woman.' Ibid, p. 178.
11 Ibid, p. 5.
12 Throughout his book, *Method and Madness*, Butscher referred to Plath as a 'bitch goddess'.
13 Charles Newman, (editor), *The Art of Sylvia Plath: A Symposium*, 1970.
14 Charles Newman, 'Candor is the only Wile', in *The Art of Sylvia Plath: A Symposium*, p. 26.
15 Robert Phillips, *The Confessional Poets*, 1973.
16 Carole Ferrier, 'The beekeeper's apprentice', in *New Views on the Poetry*, edited by Gary Lane, 1979, p. 211.
17 The 1950s saw a remarkable rise in the birth rate which peaked in 1957. In that year American women were producing children at a rate unmatched since before the First World War.
18 William O'Neill, *The Years of Confidence 1945–1960*, 1986, p. 40.
19 Jacqueline Rose, op. cit., p. 8.
20 Judith Kroll, *Chapters in a Mythology: The Poetry of Sylvia Plath*, 1976.
21 Jacqueline Rose, op. cit., p. 10.
22 Roland Barthes, 'The Death of the Author', in *The Rustle of Language*, translated by Richard Howard, Basil Blackwell, Oxford, 1986, p. 49.
23 Sylvia Plath, 'Words', in *Collected Poems*, edited by Ted Hughes, 1981. A conversation in 1985 with the owners of the house in Fitzroy Road in which Plath lived up to her death revealed that in their opinion Plath had written at least one other poem, 'Three Sycamores', the title referring to the trees in her back garden.

24 Seamus Heaney, 'The indefatigable hoof-taps', *The Times Literary Supplement*, 5–11 February, 1988, pp. 134 and 143; Eric Homberger, 'Sylvia Plath: a life under the bell jar', *The Times Higher Education Supplement*, 11 March, 1988, p. 17; A Alvarez, *The Savage God*, 1971; Ronald Hayman, *The Death and Life of Sylvia Plath*, 1991, and 'Poetry of life and hate', *The Independent*, 3 March 1988. p.16; Alan Brownjohn, 'A way out of the mind', *The Times Literary Supplement*, 12 February 1982, p. 165; Peter Porter, 'Collecting Her Strength', *New Statesman* No. LXXXI, 4 June 1971, pp. 774–5, and Review of Hayman and Rose, BBC Radio 4, Kaleidoscope, 1991; Michael Horowitz, 'Plathitudes and Plathology', *The Times Saturday Review*, 22 June, 1991, p. 23.

25 In an article written for the *London Magazine*, Plath considered the 'real issues' of her time to be '. . . the issues of every time – the hurt and wonder of loving; making in all its forms – children, loaves of bread, paintings, buildings; and the conservation of life of all people in all places, the jeopardizing of which no abstract doubletalk of "peace" or "implacable foes" can excuse.' Sylvia Plath, 'Context' in *Johnny Panic and the Bible of Dreams*, edited by Ted Hughes, 1977, p. 98.

Chapter 2.

1 Adrienne Rich 'When We Dead Awaken: Writing as Re-Vision', in *On Lies, Secrets and Silence*, 1980, p. 36.

2 During her guest editorship for *Mademoiselle* magazine, Plath interviewed both Marianne Moore and Elizabeth Bishop.

3 Editor's Note, *Journals*, p. XIII.

4 *Journals*, p. 23. There are a number of references in the *Journals* to what appear to be erotic relationships with women, for example p. 55, p. 63, p. 301, and p. 303.

5 A collage by Plath in the possession of the Neilson

Library at Smith in one corner depicts a man and woman sleeping with matching sleeping masks, the caption reading: 'It's "HIS and HER Time" all over America.'

6 Plath's first novel *Hill of Leopards*, which she intended to dedicate to her husband, also had a romantic view of heterosexual relations:

> about an American girl finding her soul in a year (or, rather, nine Fulbright months) at Cambridge and on the Continent. It will be very controversial as I intend to expose a lot of people and places. And start my new gospel, which is as old as native rituals, about the positive acceptance of conflict and uncertainty and pain as the soil for true knowledge and life. (*LH* p. 311.)

Unfortunately in mid-1962 during a visit by her mother, Plath, suspecting her husband of infidelity, took the manuscript of this novel into the garden and burnt it. (See Aurelia Schober Plath, 'Sylvia Plath's Letters Home – some reflections by her mother', *The Listener*, 22 April 1976, p. 515–16.)

7 Editor's note, *CP*, p. 295. *Ariel* is still being published in the edition chosen by Ted Hughes.

8 Not for nothing has Plath been acclaimed by the feminist critic Ellen Moers: 'No writer has meant more to the current feminist movement, though Plath was hardly a "movement" person and she died at age thirty before it began.' (*Literary Women*, 1978, p. XIII.)

9 'Three Women' (*CP*, pp. 176–87) is a prime example.

10 It links up with the traditional view of relations between the sexes being in continuous conflict. In 'Getting There', (CP, pp. 247–9), a poem which deals with this issue, the speaker exclaims wearily that 'it is some war or other'.

11 Plath focuses very cleverly on male violence in *The Bell Jar* in a scene of attempted rape. Esther remarks perceptively: 'I began to see why women-haters could

make such fools of women. Women-haters were like gods; invulnerable and chock-full of power'.

12 Popular literature of the 1950s portrayed the American woman in various different guises, as, for instance, a 'spoiled princess', an emotional cripple, as Mom or Supermom. (See P A Carter *Another Part of the Fifties*, 1983, p. 90.)

13 The language here is the parlance of a magician. But this is performance art with a difference!

14 Having broken her leg in a skiing accident, *The Bell Jar's* heroine Esther warded off the temptation of ascribing this to an external cause, such as her boyfriend Buddy Willard, who had urged her to try out on the slope without adequate training or preparation. 'Every time it rained the old leg-break seemed to remember itself, and what it remembered was a dull hurt. Then I thought, "Buddy Willard made me break that leg". Then I thought, "No, I broke it myself, I broke it on purpose to pay myself back for being such a heel".' *The Bell Jar*, p. 90.

15 'The Beekeeper's Daughter' (*CP*, p. 118) in particular provides a Freudian perspective on the relationship by indicating the sexual undertones of the father-daughter relationship. As Susan van Dyne has commented: 'The opulent engulfing sexuality of the female bees exceeds the aging father's capacity to match it. He is an inadequate bridegroom for the queen bee, still he dominates it.' Susan van Dyne, 'More terrible than she ever was: The Manuscripts of Sylvia Plath's Bee Poems', Smith College, Library Rare Book Room, 1982, p. 9.

16 Plath, quoted in A Alvarez 'Sylvia Plath', in *The Modern Poet: Essays from The Review*, edited by Ian Hamilton, 1962, p. 81. Her preoccupation with this theme also derived from her interest in psychology, which at one point she had considered taking a doctorate in (*Journals*, p. 283), and which she was able to enjoy during her work as secretary/receptionist in the Massachusetts General Hospital.

17 Another of Plath's wry puns.

18 Hesther Eisenstein, *Contemporary Feminist Thought*, 1984, p. 138.
19 The likelihood that the lover in this poem is male is indicated by the lines 'Not you, nor him/Not him, nor him' and by the reference to sex as pain: 'Your body/Hurts me as the world hurts God.'
20 The poem is another of Plath's many sophisticatedly witty pastiches on the subject of sex, this time with a reference to the passion of Christ.
21 The female speaker achieves her emancipation through leaving behind her relations with men, asserting her separateness from the former roles/selves she played.
22 *Journals*, p. 288. Lesbianism was an issue that interested her thematically. For her novel *The Bell Jar* she 'read the sensationalist trash which is *Nightwood* [a popular novel of the 1950s] – all perverts, all ranting, melodramatic: "The sex that God forgot" – self-pity, like the stage whine of the Dream Play. Pity us: Oh, Oh, Oh: Mankind is pitiable . . .' (*Journals*, p. 205.) 'I imagined the situation of two lesbians: the one winning a woman with child from an apparently happy marriage. Why is it impossible to think of two women living together without lesbianism being the solution, the motive?' (*Journals*, p. 329.)
23 *BJ*, p. 231.
24 *LH*, p. 65; p. 136.
25 *Journals*, p. 259.
26 *Journals*, p. 293.
27 *Journals*, p. 197.
28 *Journals*, p. 55; p. 63; p. 301.
29 The rose is a symbol for Venus, the goddess of love.
30 In 'Wintering' Plath provides a feminist image and statement which was to be echoed later in the poetry of Adrienne Rich and other women's writing in the 1960s: 'The woman, still at her knitting,/At the cradle of Spanish walnut,/Her body a bulb in the cold and too dumb to think.' The poem shows a woman beginning to reverse the social and political passivity women had endured through the centuries.

31 Paula Bennet's book, *Emily Dickinson: Woman Poet*, 1990, for instance, focuses on Emily Dickinson's love for women as a strong positive force in her work.

32 'When such a man, bent on refusing to hear what is said, comes upon a passionate poem addressed clearly to "she" or "her", he twists logic to explain what is to him inexplicable . . . He asserts on no authority that the authentic version is addressed to "he" or "him".' Introduction to *The World Split Open: Four Centuries of Women Poets in England and America 1551–1950*, edited by Louise Bernikow, 1979, p. 15.

33 In the few instances when the speaker is male, irony is used to attack him for some moral failing, and this is not the case in this poem.

34 Correspondence between the Plath Estate and Faber and Faber, conveyed to the author, summer 1992.

35 Interestingly, in Plath's recording of this poem she stresses the first five words of this line. *Sylvia Plath Reading Her Poetry, Great American Poets*, 1987.

36 'Stones' denotes a death-like state.

37 Plath's description of the attic room is a clever take-off of stylised lesbian salons of the 1920s and 1930s, epitomised in *Nightwood*.

38 The title is an obvious allusion to the island Lesbos and its most famous writer Sappho, whom Plath regarded as a rival (*Journals*, p. 211), and after whom she named her cat. (*LH*, p. 350.)

39 This image connects 'Lesbos' to its antecedent 'Leaving Early' with similar dress code imagery.

40 That is, the husband who has become a prisoner of his sexuality: 'He is hugging his ball and chain down by the gate/That opens to the sea/Where it drives in, white and black/Then spews it back.' The sexual imagery is apparent. The situation here is reminiscent of one Plath describes in her *Journals* in 1959, where she left two of her friends together, 'yet felt like a brown-winged moth around a rather meager candle flame, drawn'. (*Journals*, p. 301.)

41 This contrasts neatly with the puns elsewhere in the poem, as her friend is described like a piece of meat

in her willingness to fake orgasm: 'In New York, in Hollywood, the men said:' "Through?/Gee baby, you are rare".'

42 This was very much Plath's own experience, even with her closest friends. A passage in the *Journals* refers to a meeting with her old college friend and alter ego, Marcia: 'She shells some resentment under her brisk breezy talk, I am too simple to call it envy: "Do all your students think you're just wonderful and traveled and a writer?" Acid baths. Given time . . . I'll attack her next year and get at her good innards. Innocence my mask. It always was, in her eyes . . . I the great dreamy unsophisticated and helpless thus challenging lout-girl.' (*Journals*, p. 187.)

43 My italics.

44 'Acids' links this poem to the later 'Lesbos' where 'the potatoes hiss' and the lover is 'A vase of acid'. This eerily echoes Plath's earlier prediction in her Journals, when she wrote on this subject: 'I desire the things which will destroy me in the end.' (*Journals*, p. 22.)

45 This idea was suggested by Judith Kroll. Plath believed in D H Lawrence's notion of passion as a force that had to destroy the old, rotten self in order to create the real and authentic person: '. . . Ran to catch Krook . . . who went on to D H Lawrence & incredible fable: *The Man Who Died*. She read sections, felt chilled, as in last paragraph of "The Dead", as if angel had hauled me by the hair in a shiver of gooseflesh: about the temple of Isis bereaved, Isis in search. Lawrence died in Vence, where I had my mystic vision with Sassoon; I was the woman who died, and I came in touch through Sassoon that spring [with] that flaming of life, that resolute fury of existence.' (*Journals*, p. 128.)

46 Plath was at this time learning to ride bareback over the Yorkshire moors.

47 My italics. The sexual connotations of 'furrow' and 'neck' make it clear that this is interaction between women: 'furrow' is a metaphor for the vagina and 'neck' a metaphor for the cervix.

48 Plath's use of 'glitter' in this poem, while immediately

appropriate to the context, stands also in direct contrast to the use of it in two later poems, 'Berck-Plage' and 'Death & Co.', where deceptive appearances are conjured up, rather than the authentic relations evident in 'Ariel'. 'Seas' is an example of Plath's frequent and sophisticated use of puns, this one being based on her German studies at that time, which was the language of her parents; in German 'sie' is the feminine plural of 'she'.

49 This image is echoed in 'The Couriers' (*CP*, p. 247), written several days later, where art is 'the immaculate cauldron'. Significantly, the horse in 'Ariel' is also a symbol for energy on all levels. (See Tom Chetwynd, *A Dictionary of Symbols*, 1982, p. 206.) The same erotic wordplay occurs in 'Eavesdropper' written in October and December 1962 (*CP*, pp. 260–1), a poem which Ted Hughes informs us 'was written in slightly longer form on 15 October 1962, but reduced to its present length, by simple deletions, on 31 December. No final copy was made.' (*CP*, p. 294. Editor's note.)

50 M D Uroff, 'Sylvia Plath on Motherhood', *The Midwest Quarterly*, 1973, p. 70. Plath saw herself very much as a tripartite achiever. After her marriage in 1956 she expressed hopes that her husband would want to settle in the USA, where life was materially so much easier, since 'if I want to keep on being as triple-threat woman: wife, writer, teacher (to be swapped later for motherhood, I hope) I can't be a drudge, the way housewives are forced to be here.' Plath, quoted in Lois Ames, 'Notes towards a biography', in *New Views on The Poetry*, 1979, p. 166.

51 *Journals*, p. 293.

Chapter 3.

1 P R King, *Nine Contemporary Poets*, p. 169; Edward Butscher, *Sylvia Plath: Method and Madness*, p. 362.

2 This is a poem with a very clear feminist slant, which focuses on *survival*, the survival of a female community.

3 David Holbrook, *Sylvia Plath: Poetry and Existence*, 1976, p. 132.

4 David Holbrook, op. cit., p. 222.

5 Ibid, p. 111.

6 This is reminiscent of a passage in *The Bell Jar*, describing an experience the heroine Esther has: 'the longer I lay there in the clear hot water the purer I felt, and when I stepped out at last and wrapped myself in one of the big, soft, white, hotel bath-towels I felt pure and sweet as a new baby.' (*The Bell Jar*, p. 22.)

7 This image is also the central one in *The Bell Jar*, in which mental illness is regarded as a 'bell jar', distorting the outside world.

8 David Holbrook, op. cit., p. 111.

9 Sylvia Plath, Note, *CP*, p. 294.

10 So death, like everything else, has become a form of entertainment in a world where values have been turned upside down.

11 This is the negative side of the 'world community', created by the mass media.

12 David Holbrook, op. cit., p. 19.

13 The fire, with its connotations of warmth and intensity, is a symbol of the life-force, which appears in the guise of the 'little hell flames', the poppies in 'Poppies in July' (*CP*, p. 203), and also in the 'red/Eye, the cauldron of morning', the source of creativity in 'Ariel' (*CP*, pp. 239–40).

14 In the poem 'Two Campers in Cloud Country' (*CP*, pp. 144–5) nature as a healing force also appears as 'Lethe'.

15 'To get there' is a colloquial expression meaning 'to succeed'. Plath nowhere in her work refers to death as an achievement, and there are no indications that she equates dying with 'getting there' in this poem.

16 It is a positive destination, a time for taking stock of the old and for starting afresh.

17 Annette Lavers, 'The World as Icon – on Sylvia Plath's Themes', in *The Art of Sylvia Plath*, 1970, p. 128.

18 The imagery of this poem invites comparison with

ilia' (*CP*, pp. 258–9), with its description of grotesque machine-like angels: 'These people ...ith torsos of steel,/Winged elbows and eyeholes.' The 'pure, acetylene virgin' seems like some bizarre prototype of Frankenstein's bride as depicted in the classic expressionist horror films. Purity is also by no means something to be commended 'Pure? What does it mean' is the first revealing line of the poem. One verse of this poem, missing from the published version but broadcast in Plath's recording of it ('The Poet Speaks', London: Argos Records, 1965) refers to the Spanish Inquisition and the double standards then prevalent, together with the 1950s morality. Plath's conclusion is that purity is very much a characteristic feature of a hypocritical society.

19 The sexual connotations are obvious here.

20 The acceptance of life with its imperfections and suffering was also central to Plath's philosophy: 'I am true to the essence of myself, and I know who that self is . . . and will live with her through sorrow and pain, singing all the way, even in anguish and grief, the triumph of love over death and sickness and war and all the flaws of my dear world . . .' *LH*, p. 243.

21 The tulips with their vitality are comparable to the train, the 'slow/Horse', a metaphor for the life-force in 'Sheep in Fog'. (*CP*, p. 262.)

22 Joyce Carol Oates, 'The death throes of romanticism,' *Southern Review*, Vol. 9, No. 3, 1973, p. 519.

23 Sigmund Freud, *An Outline of Psychoanalysis*, 1940. Freud believed that there was a fundamental tension underlying all existence, which was the struggle between Eros – love – and Thanatos – death.

24 'This is the light of the mind, cold and planetary', Plath wrote in 'The Moon and the Yew Tree' (*CP*, pp. 172–3) in 1961. Throughout her life she was wary of the overly, arid intellectual life led by the people she had studied with at Smith and Cambridge. Her poetry warns against over-intellectualising life.

25 This is similar to a situation depicted in *The Bell Jar*,

pp. 65–66, and is based on a visit to a hospital made by Plath in the company of a medical student friend.

26 Margaret Newlin, 'The Suicide Bandwagon', *Critical Quarterly*, No. 14, 1972, p. 376.

27 A section in *Johnny Panic and the Bible of Dreams* indicates the initial biographical source for the second incident, 'Rose and Percy B', pp. 242–3.

28 See *CP*, p. 293.

29 Sylvia Plath, quoted in Edward Butscher, op. cit. p. 351. Ted Hughes's enigmatic note to this poem refers to an actual visit made by 'two well-meaning men who invited TH [Ted Hughes] to live abroad at a tempting salary and whom she therefore resented.' (*CP*, p. 294.)

30 In 'Ariel' the speaker 'foam[s] to wheat, a glitter of seas', while in 'Berck-Plage', in opposition to the sound of the 'dead bell', there is 'A glitter of wheat and crude earth'.

31 M L Rosenthal, 'Sylvia Plath and Confessional Poetry', in *The Art of Sylvia Plath*, 1970, p. 76.

32 Despite the at first sight ominous ending of the poem, death retains a grim face. Even the metre with its preponderance of masculine endings, 'stir', 'star', 'bell' (all ending with a stressed syllable) sounds a horrific note of finality and the final statement 'done for' stands in opposition to the making of the two faces of death. The speaker seems to have become passive, lapsing into stasis and the purified geometric shape of a star, characterising death. Yet the very notes of doom and gloom and the overly dramatised grim inevitability of death in this poem point to the use of hyperbole to deflate the ritual of death presented by the two callers.

33 David Holbrook, op. cit., p. 2.

34 Perfection is also the theme of another 1963 poem 'The Munich Mannequins' (*CP*, pp. 262–3), where it is condemned as nothing short of narcissism: 'perfection is terrible, it cannot have children.'

35 Another poem 'Kindness' (*CP*, pp. 269–70), also written at the end of Plath's life, shows how unlikely

it is that the dead woman in 'Edge' could be identified with Plath. In 'Kindness' the speaker, behind whom Plath is discernible, calls her two children 'two roses', unlike the dead woman in 'Edge', who could only regard her children as 'petals of a rose', with no independent existence of their own.

Chapter 4.

1 Louise Bernikow commented that religion was 'an acceptable subject because it focuses on the men who are God the Father and the Son, and suits patriarchal taste more subtly. The religious experience, a receiving experience, however intense, is never considered unfeminine. On the contrary.' (Introduction to *The World Split Open: Four Centuries of Women Poets in England and America 1551–1950*, 1974, p. 7.)

2 As Barbara Hardy has commented, Plath's poetry had the feminist power to subvert and disturb through her ability to show the insidious and extensive implications of patriarchal power structures. ('The Poetry of Sylvia Plath', in *Women Reading Women's Writing*, edited by Sue Roe, 1987, p. 10.)

3 *LH*, p. 201.

4 *LH*, p. 449.

5 Like Emerson Plath found much to acclaim in this religion, which rejected the doctrine of the Trinity and the divinity of Christ in favour of the unipersonality of God, with reason and conscience serving as the criteria for belief and practice. It also appealed to her by virtue of its affirmation of the abiding goodness of human nature – she was at heart a humanist – and its criticism of the doctrines of man's fall from grace, the atonement and eternal punishment.

6 *LH*, p. 449.

7 *LH*, p. 466.

8 *LH*, p. 433.

9 Wagner-Martin, *Sylvia Plath: A Biography*, 1988, p. 226.

10 E Butscher, *Sylvia Plath*: *Method and Madness*, 1976, p. 286.

11 ie *The Poetry of American Women from 1632 to 1945*, 1977, pp. 6–7. Alicia Ostriker in *Stealing the Language*, 1987, also highlighted the different responses given by women poets to religion, pp. 137–8.

12 Plath was familiar with the Theatre of the Absurd with which she was suitably impressed, especially with the work of Ionesco: 'I read four Ionesco plays: *The Bald Soprano, Jack, The Lesson, The Chairs*: terrifying and funny: playing on our old conventions and banalities and making them carried to the last extreme to show, by the discrepancy between real and real-to-the-last thrust, how funny we are and how far gone. "We eat well because we live in a suburb of London and our name is Smith." A family crisis: a boy won't submit and say he adores hashed brown potatoes: the smallness of the object contrasted with the totality of emotion involved on all sides: a ridicule, a terror.' (*Journals*, p. 282.)

13 The language used by the Trinity in this poem is genteel to the point of parody. Gentility was also one of Plath's *bête noires*.

14 The poem's title refers to the synthetically constructed capital of Brazil, its architecture completely modernist.

15 The horrific irony inherent in the perverse redemption portrayed in the poem is underscored by repetition of the last words of The Lord's Prayer.

16 The mythical kingdom of Sir Tristram in Arthurian legend.

17 *The Art of Sylvia Plath*, edited by Charles Newman, 1970, p. 117.

18 The biographical reference to Plath's own father is also valid. Curiously, this poem, perhaps the best known of all of Plath poems, is missing from the index to the *Collected Poems*.

19 Phyllis Chesler, *Women and Madness*, 1972, caption to Illustration 4, between pp. 168 and 169.

20 In a radio broadcast Plath commented that in this

poem she imagined the 'great absolutes of the philosophers gathered around the crib of a new-born baby girl who has nothing but life.' ('The Living Poet', BBC Third Programme 8 July 1961.)

21 In Plath's recording of 'Fever 103°' (though not in the published text) she includes the lines: 'O autodafe/-The purple men gold-crusted, thick with spleen/Sit with their hooks and crooks/And stoke the light.' In the poem these lines come immediately before 'The tinder cries'. On the theme of purification Plath demonstrates how Christianity's aim was 'laundering the grossness' from souls during the Inquisition and parallel incidents. ('The Poet Speaks', Argos Records, 1965). Similarly, Plath has a go at the superhumanly fastidious Catholic religion in *The Bell Jar*, as the following passages indicate: 'I collected men with interesting names. I already knew a Socrates. He was tall and ugly and intellectual and the son of some big Greek movie producer in Hollywood, but also a Catholic, which ruined it for both of us.' (*BJ*, p. 53). 'The only trouble was, Church, even the Catholic Church, didn't take up the whole of your life. No matter how much you knelt and prayed, you still had to eat three meals a day and have a job and live in the world.' (*BJ*, p. 174). 'My Aunt Libby's husband had made a joke once, about a nun that a nunnery sent to Teresa for a check-up. This nun kept hearing harp notes in her ears and a voice saying over and over, "Alleluia!" Only she wasn't sure, on being closely questioned, whether the voice was saying Alleluia or Arizona. The nun had been born in Arizona. I think she ended up in some asylum.' (*BJ*, p. 175). '. . . I imagined myself going to some Boston priest – it would have to be Boston, because I didn't want any priest in my home town to know I'd thought of killing myself. Priests were terrible gossips.' (*BJ*, p. 174).

22 As Ann Oakley has commented:

women's religious orders considerably facilitated the participation of women in public life in the

period up to the end of the sixteenth century. . . .
The substitution of Parliament for the Church and
the monarchy as the governing body of the land
may have abolished hereditary supremacy but it
entrenched sexual supremacy . . . (Ann Oakley,
Subject Women, 1981, p. 5.)

23 The poem 'Sheep in Fog' (*CP*, p. 262) revolves around
an absence of something to believe in. The title alludes
ironically to the speaker, who is a member of a flock
caught up in a world devoid of faith. The images of
this poem connect with an earlier poem, written in
1961 by Adrienne Rich, entitled 'Apology' (published
in *Snapshots of a Daughter-in-Law*, 1970, p. 50). In
this poem the speaker is equally confused: 'Today,
turning/in the fog of my mind,/I knew, the thing I
really/couldn't stand in the house/is a woman/with a
mindful of fog/ and bloodletting claws/and the nerves
of a bird/and the nightmares of a dog.'

24 Throughout her life Plath was fascinated by the supernatural and she believed in her intuitive powers. In
Yorkshire, with her husband, she visited a local witch,
a visit they both found disappointingly uneventful.
E Butscher, op. cit., p. 192. On frequent occasions
she used tarot cards and a ouija board.

25 Plath's note on the poem shows how the yew tree was
its most dominant symbol: 'The yew tree was just
too proud to be a passing black mark.' (Note, *CP*,
p. 292.)

26 Similarly, in 'The Moon and the Yew Tree' there are
'trees of the mind', assigned the unflattering and
ominous colour black.

27 With her rejection of what she regarded as the
hypocritical comfort and superficiality of religious
ritual, Plath showed her way of thinking to be similar
to that of the existential writer and philosopher Albert
Camus, with whose work she was familiar, especially
to his hero Meursault in *L'étranger* (published in 1957)
who, facing death, refuses the priest's absolution in a
last act of defiance (pp. 175–78).

28 The poem 'Totem' also dispenses with the intellectual and religious images of worship, that is, Plato and Christ.

29 Plath and Hughes considered that through the ouija board they had managed to contact their own spirit, 'Pan', about whom Plath wrote 'Dialogue over a Ouija Board' (*CP*, pp. 276–87) 'using the actual "spirit" text of one of the ouija sessions' (*CP*, p. 276). Before moving into Yeats's house in Primrose Hill, Plath tried to get in touch with his spirit, believing that she had established contact with him when she visited his tower in Ireland: 'I opened a book of his plays in front of Susan as a joke for a "message" and read, "Get wine and food to give you strength and courage, and I will get the house ready".' (*LH*, p. 480.)

30 Plath's personal library contained works by Nietzsche, Kafka, Ortega y Gasset and Paul Tillich, now on display at the Neilson Library, Smith College. Plath's mysticism connected her to two of her favourite poets, Blake and Wordsworth. In her address book, now in the Sylvia Plath Collection at the Rare Book Room, Neilson Library, Smith College, there are references to 'St Theresa during delirium' and to the Revelation of St John, Chapter 12, Verse 3 ('And another portent appeared in heaven; behold, a great red dragon, with seven heads and ten horns, and seven diadems on his heads.' – The Bible, Revised Standard Version, 1971, p. 234). This interest was shared with one of her favourite writers, D H Lawrence, who had written a reinterpretation of the Book of Revelation (*Apocalypse*, 1931, p. 3.)

31 Wagner–Martin, p. 186; *LH*, p. 391.

32 John MacQuarrie, *Existentialism*, 1987, p. 263.

33 This is very much in line with the Sartrean idea that man is a dynamic being who creates himself through action, through immersing himself in the nothingness at the heart of his being. (J P Sartre, *Being and Nothingness*, 1981.)

34 Eileen Aird, *Sylvia Plath*, 1973, p. 67.

35 Plath's similarity to D H Lawrence is apparent

here. As Sheila McLeod has commented, Lawrence's 'deepest and most enduring belief' was 'the courage to value life for itself with all its pain and darkness as well as its joy and enlightenment, affirming again and again in the face of nihilism and philistinism that life is meaningful and valuable, if only we are brave enough to bring meaning and value to it.' (*Men and Women*, 1985, p. 254.)

36 Lynne Salop has commented that 'Sylvia's language . . . is not so much communication as communion. It is a language in which is found a deep and authentic knowledge of what is involved in the life of free men; a language that invites us to re-enter what Martin Buber calls "the world of I and Thou".' (*Suisong*, 1978, p. 26.)

37 As the theologian John MacQuarrie has commented: 'Existentialism when developed ontologically does in fact suggest new possibilities for a concept of God, perhaps more viable than the concept of traditional theism'; . . . in the Old Testament, we hear of man compounded of the dust of the ground and the breath of life . . . [these images recur throughout Plath's poetry]. Existentialism offers a new and better model, and an updated terminology for expressing the biblical understanding of man. For instance, the "dust of the ground" may be understood as facticity [existential awareness of one's own being as a fact that is to be accepted, [p. 190] and the "breath of life" as possibility, and the ancient story receives a new intelligibility.' (*Existentialism*, 1987, p. 252 and pp. 272–3.)

Chapter 5.

1 The almost exclusive attention to *The Bell Jar* as being the only work of Plath's with any humour calls again into question the problem of biographical criticism, as critics have tended to focus their attention on what they regard as an autobiographical work, rather than on the poetry.

2 In a broadcast for a BBC radio series on Americans living in Britain, Plath showed a keen sense of humour at the sights, noting the 'taxi cabs being black and rather like large, impressive hearses'; the inclement weather was also noted: 'The weather infects me [laughs] – affects me – I say infects me – it really does infect me'; and the unexpected displays in butcher shops, was also remarked on, a new phenomenon for the supermarket-educated Plath: 'pigs kept turning themselves off and on'. 'A World of Sound', Home Service Broadcast, 7 September 1962.

3 In a letter to her mother in 1956 Plath wrote: 'My whole session with Dr B is responsible for making me a rich, well-balanced, humorous, easy-going person, with a joy in the daily life, including all its imperfections: sinus, weariness, furstration, and all those other niggling things that we all have to bear.' (*LH*, p. 215.)

4 It was an aim which remained important for her throughout her life. In a letter written five months before her death after she and her husband had separated, Plath wrote of how she intended to be a humorous novelist: 'I think I'll be a pretty good novelist, very funny – my stuff makes me laugh and laugh, and if I can laugh now it must be hellishly funny stuff.' (*LH*, p. 467.)

5 *LH*, pp. 168–9.

6 Interview with Sylvia Plath by Lee Anderson 1958 (quoted in J D McClatchy, 'Short Circuits and Folding Mirrors', in *Sylvia Plath: New Views on the Poetry*, edited by Gary Lane, 1979). In a *Journal* note in the summer of 1951 she referred to her writing as being close to 'the whimsical, lyrical, typographically eccentric verse of E E Cummings . . .' (p. 32.)

7 'A World of Sound', op. cit., 1962.

8 In a letter to her mother she wrote of her acting performance in a farce at Cambridge, where she was a member of the university theatre group: '. . . my dear, adorable play director gave me the ultimate laurel today by saying that my performance was

"excruciatingly funny" and doubling up with laughter. I was so happy, because the part of this mad poetess, Phoebe Clinkett, is rather absurd farce and depends on a kind of double entendre slanting of words and gestures which I tried today, having just learned my part, 15 flighty, rather verbose speeches . . .' (*LH*, p. 190.)

9 For example, Helen Vendler, 'An Intractable Metal', in *The Atlantic Monthly*, May 1982, p. 131.

10 Barbara Hardy, 'The Poetry of Sylvia Plath', in *The Survival of Poetry*, edited by Martin Dodsworth, 1974.

11 Sylvia Plath, Recording of 'Fever 103°', in 'The Poet Speaks', Argos Records, London 1965.

12 P R King, *Nine Contemporary Poets*, 1979, p. 87.

13 Marjorie Perloff, 'Angst and Animism in the Poetry of Sylvia Plath', *Journal of Modern Literature*, 1970, p. 64.

14 In a collage Plath made up, now in the possession of the Neilson Library Smith College, there is at first sight an odd assortment of images – a smiling but sinister Eisenhower in the centre, the most imposing figure, a badge entitled SLEEP on his jacket, an open pack of cards in his hand, with an upside-down caption reading CHANGE YOUR THINKING; Nixon half-lurking behind curtains to his right; above Eisenhower's head there is the most advanced military jet of its time aiming its hardware at the nether regions of a woman in a bathing costume, the caption reading EVERY MAN WANTS A WOMAN ON A PEDESTAL. At the foot of her pedestal is a tube of Rheingold's extra dry hand lotion, symbolic of her future duties; in the upper left-hand part of the collage, men and women with sleeping masks slumber next to a caption 'It's HIS and HER Time all over America . . .', while to their right two grown men play with a racing set; at the lower right-hand corner, a middle-aged woman stands, slumped forward and diminutive with respect to the other figures in the collage; the caption beside her reads 'FATIGUE BUILD-UP . . . America's growing health hazard'. Irony

and hyperbole are the key humouristic tools in this collage, spiced by a fair helping of the accoutrements of black humour and *film noir*. These were techniques Plath used generously in her poetry.

15 Alicia Ostriker, 'Fact as Style: The Americanization of Sylvia', in *Language and Style*, No. 1 1968, p. 209.

16 B Hardy, op. cit., p. 218.

17 In a letter to her mother she characterised a don at Cambridge: 'I see in Cambridge, particularly among the women dons, a series of such grotesques! It is almost like a caricature series from Dickens to see our head table at Newnham. Daily we rather merciless and merry Americans, South Africans, and Scottish students remark the types at the dons' table, which range from a tall, cadaverous woman with purple hair (really!) to a midget Charles Addams fat creature who has to stand on a stool to get into the soup tureen.' (*LH*, p. 198.)

18 Plath's poetry teems with the paraphernalia of the Gothic: ghosts in 'All the Dead Dears' (*CP*, pp. 70–1), 'The Ghost's Leavetaking' (*CP*, pp. 90–1), the monstrous muse 'bald' with 'no eyes' in 'The Tour' (*CP*, pp. 237–8), cauldrons in 'Ariel' (*CP*, pp. 239–40), strange invisible messengers in 'The Couriers' (*CP*, p. 247), and many other sensational and supernatural occurrences.

19 S Gubar, and S M Gilbert, *The Madwoman in the Attic*, 1979, p. 85.

20 She enjoyed the work of Ionesco, as she says in *Journals*, p. 283. A passage from a letter describing a walk taken to Grantchester by herself and her husband reveals a strong sense of the absurd:

> You'd laugh, but I'm going to put this scene into my novel [*Hill of Leopards*, presumably, which she later destroyed]. We began mooing at a pasture of cows, and they all looked up, and, as if hypnotized, began to follow us in a crowd of about twenty across the pasture to a wooden stile, staring, fascinated. I stood on the stile and, in a resonant voice, recited

all I knew of Chaucer's *Canterbury Tales* for about twenty minutes. I never had such an intelligent, fascinated audience. You should have seen their expressions as they came flocking up around me. I'm sure they loved it! (*LH*, p. 307.)

Chapter 6.

1 Parodying 'the iron law of "togetherness"', Plath made up a collage, now in the possession of the Rare Book Room, Smith College, Library. Among the items on display for consumption Plath included a figure of a woman in a bathing suit, targeted by the latest military jet, with a caption 'EVERY MAN WANTS HIS WOMAN ON A PEDESTAL'. Consumerism was part of the ethos of the decade. As the historian Paul Carter commented: 'In World War Two America had taken it for granted that the armed forces had had to waste things in order to win the war. Now, in the fifties, there was no war; yet the need continued to consume things, less theatrically but no less thoroughly than in war's fountaining explosions. If we didn't, people told each other, we would fall right back into the economic depression from which the war had rescued us.' (*Another Part of the Fifties*, 1983, p. 40.)

Adlai Stevenson's graduation address to Smith College in 1955 stressed how women graduating, who were among the most talented in the country, should concentrate on being good homemakers for their husbands.

2 Plath's father had studied to become a Lutheran minister, but subsequently chose to abandon this profession, becoming instead a Professor of Entomology. Plath's family life revolved around a Puritan work ethic, which led Sylvia Plath to comment in 1957: 'I think that through our years of family scraping to get money and scholarships, etc., we three [herself, her mother

185

and brother] developed an almost Puritan sense that being 'lazy' and spending money on luxuries like meals out or theater or travel was slightly wicked.' (*LH*, pp. 309–11.)

3 *LH*, p. 162.
4 *LH*, p. 304.
5 *LH*, p. 163.
6 *Journals*, p. 81. Plath was wary of America's cold-war mentality and refused to regard the Soviets as 'the enemy'; she met Bulganin and Khrushchev at a reception in New York's Claridge Hotel, an occasion which reinforced her pacifist beliefs. 'Had several, short, good talks with Russian officers who were learning English, even mentioned Dostoevsky and ended up toasting Russo-American relations in vodka with a charming blond chap working in commerce: both of us agreeing that if we could meet each other as simple people who wanted to have families and jobs and a good life, there would never be any wars, because we would make such good friends.' (*LH*, p. 242.)
7 D H Lawrence, *Fantasia of the Unconscious and Psychoanalysis and the Unconscious*, 1977, p. 169; Virginia Woolf, *Three Guineas*, 1977.
8 Wendy Martin, 'God's Lioness – Sylvia Plath: Her Prose and Poetry', in *Women's Studies*, 1971, Vol. 1, p. 195.
9 David Meakin, *Man & Work*, 1976, p. 11 n.
10 Rollo May, *The Courage to Create*, 1975, p. 70.
11 *Journals*, p. 31. The existential theologian Paul Tillich had warned in the 1950s that one of the greatest temptations for people living in industrial societies, where everyone was involved in the process of mechanical production and consumption, was to treat others as objects. (Paul Tillich, *The Courage to Be*, 1952.)
12 This is the negative effect of Marshall McLuhan's ideal of the 'global village'. (*The Medium is the Massage*, 1967.)
13 Reminiscent of Ortega y Gasset's 'herd'. The 'vampiric crowd' is the result *ad absurdum* of the kind of peer-group pressure which dominated the 1950s. In

her personal library Plath had David Riesman's *The Lonely Crowd: A Study of the Changing American Character* (published in 1950). Writing on the power of the peer-group, Riesman commented: 'The peer-group becomes the measure of all things; the individual has no defenses the group cannot batter down. In this situation the competitive drives for achievement sponsored in children by the remnants of inner-direction in their parents come into conflict with the cooperative demands sponsored by the peer-group. The child therefore is forced to rechannel the competitive drive for achievement, as demanded by the parent, into his drive for approval from the peers.' (p. 83.)

14 Interestingly, the sex of the applicant seems irrelevant.

15 In comparison to the applicant! Plath's reading of this poem is appropriately cynical and acerbic. ('Spoken Arts Treasury of 100 Modern Poets Reading their poems', Vol. 18, 1957.)

An earlier poem 'The Goring' (1956, *CP*, p. 47) pinpointed the depravity of consumerist pleasures. The bullfight, in its dreariness, 'Cumbrous routine, not artwork', is transformed in an act of poetic justice as the bullfighter makes a fatal error. The spectacle then becomes art: 'The whole act formal, fluent as a dance/Blood faultlessly broached redeemed the sullied air, the earth's grossness.'

16 'The Tour' has the same tongue-in-cheek, sharp style as Stevie Smith's work, whom Plath admired.

17 An appropriate choice of words; this is a machine which defies expectations.

18 The intensity of Celan's poetry and his declamatory style are strikingly similar to Plath's and his work has often been compared to hers, although it lacked Plath's breadth of vision. Plath's poetry has also been compared to the poetry of Nelly Sachs: 'There is perhaps something in the thought that the worse and the more direct the experience the more right one may feel one has if one recovers, to take horror for granted and to construct something positive – to

feel that the dead impose a duty to live rather than a duty to mourn.' (*British Poetry since 1960*, edited by Michael Schmidt and Grevel Lindop, 1972, p. 221.)

19 *LH*, p. 467.

20 An earlier poem 'The Thin People' (1957, *CP*, pp. 64–5) takes up the theme of the unfathomable scale of horror and the bleak bequest of the presence of those murdered to their descendants, who are powerless to shake off their feelings of guilt. This idea runs through 'All the Dead Dears' (1957, *CP*, pp. 70–1) and 'The Ghost's Leavetaking' (1958, *CP*, pp. 90–1).

21 *LH*, p. 284.

22 *LH*, p. 377.

23 *JP*, p. 98.

24 LH, pp. 437–8.

25 Krupp was implicated in the mass-murder mechanisms of the death-camps in the Second World War.

26 In her introduction to this poem Plath imagined the two faces of death as 'two men, two business friends who have come to call'. (Note, *CP*, p. 294.)

27 Carole Ferrier, 'The Beekeeper's Apprentice', in *New Views on the Poetry*, edited by Gary Lane, 1979 pp. 203–17. Plath's use of bee imagery links her with existential writers such as Ortega y Gasset, whose book *The Revolt of the Masses* she possessed, and with the existential philosopher Karl Jaspers whose statement on the masses Plath reflected in her poetry:

'The rule of the masses affects the activities and habits of the individual. It has become obligatory to fulfil a function which shall in some way be regarded as useful to the masses. The masses and their apparatus are the objects of our most vital interest. The masses are our masters; and for everyone who looks facts in the face his existence has become dependent on them, so that the thought of them must control his doings, his cares and his duties. Even an articulated mass always tends to become unspiritual and inhuman. It is life without existence, superstition without faith. It may stamp

all flat; it is disinclined to tolerate independence and
greatness, but prone to constrain people to become
as automatic as ants.'

Karl Jaspers, (*Man in the Modern Age*, Routledge,
London, 1951, p. 43)

28 *Sylvia Plath: A Biography*, Linda Wagner-Martin,
   1988 p. 59.
29 LH, p. 378.
30 *LH*, p. 284.
31 Adrienne Rich, 'Conditions for Work', in *On Lies,
   Secrets and Silence – Selected Prose 1966–1978*, 1979,
   p. 207.
32 'Ocean 1212-W', in *JP*, p. 123.
33 *LH*, p. 284.
34 LH, p. 284.
35 *LH*, p. 256.
36 In *The Complete Poems of D H Lawrence*, 1964,
   pp. 349–50.
37 *JP*, p. 98.
38 In 'Berck-Plage' (*CP*, pp. 196–201) the speaker feels
   impotent regarding the compassion she feels towards
   the disabled children she sees, walking on the beach
   'with hooks and cries'. Her heart is 'too small to
   bandage their terrible faults'.
39 Sylvia Plath introducing a selection of her own poems
   read by herself and Marion Kane. 'The Living Poet',
   BBC Third Programme, 8 July 1961.
40 Alicia Ostriker, *Stealing the Language*, 1987, p. 118.

Chapter 7.

1 Ted Hughes, 'Ariel', *Poetry Book Society*, 1965. Bulletin, No. 44, February 1965, p. 12.
2 Sylvia Plath, quoted in Anthony Thwaite, 'Out of the
   Quarrel: On Sylvia Plath', *Encounter* No. LIII, August
   1979, p. 66. In a letter to her mother written in 1956
   (*LH*, p. 211) Plath said: 'The important thing is the
   aesthetic form given to my chaotic experience, which
   is, as it was for James Joyce, my kind of religion, and as

necessary for me . . . as the confession and absolution for a Catholic in church.'

3   Robert Lowell, Foreword to the American edition of *Ariel*, published by Harper & Row in 1965.

4   Sylvia Plath, quoted in J D McClatchy, 'Short Circuits and Folding Mirrors', in *New Views on the Poetry*, edited by Gary Lane 1979, p. 21. In *The Colossus* Plath demonstrated her expertise in a range of verse forms: terza rima in 'Sow', 'Lorelei', 'Full Fathom Five', 'Man in Black', 'Snakecharmer' and 'Medallion', rime royale in 'The Eye-Mote', couplets in 'The Thin People' and three line a rhyme stanza in 'The Bull of Bendylaw'.

5   Ted Hughes, 'Notes on the Chronological Order of Sylvia Plath's Poems', in Charles Newman, *The Art of Sylvia Plath: A Symposium*, 1970, p. 192.

6   Sylvia Plath, quoted in *The Poet Speaks* (No. 18), Talk with Peter Orr, recorded 30 October 1962 by the British Council.

7   Sylvia Plath, quoted in Anthony Thwaite, op. cit., 1979, p. 42.

8   Margaret Noel Scarborough's thesis 'Songs of Eleusis: The Quest for Self in the Poetry of Sylvia Plath, Anne Sexton and Adrienne Rich' (University of Michigan, 1978) traces the development of the Demeter-Persephone myth; her interpretation of Plath's work casts her as a poor relation of what she sees as successful feminist writing, such as that provided by Adrienne Rich.

9   Ted Hughes, Note, *CP*, p. 287.

10 *CP*, p. 289.

11 Plath recognised only too well that the very ornateness of the literary allusions she used in her early poems prevented them from making a strong impact. As she reflected in the poem 'Stillborn' (*CP*, p. 142): 'They are proper in shape and number and every part./They sit so nicely in the pickling fluid!/They smile and smile and smile and smile at me./And still the lungs won't fill and the heart won't start.'

12 Medea in Greek mythology was the priestess of Hecate

who helped Jason to win the Golden Fleece, then married him. Subsequently he betrayed her, following which she killed her sons.

13 Plath's rejection of artificial symbols occurred contemporaneously with her rejection of conformity.

14 Plath used this as an example of what she began to see as the malevolence of God.

15 *CP*, p. 287.

16 *CP*, p. 287.

17 She regarded her husband and herself as potentially 'better than Mr and Mrs Yeats.' (who used to practice on boards) *LH*, p. 280.

18 Similarly, through much of her poetry, in particular the later poems such as 'Lady Lazarus' (*CP*, pp. 244–7) and 'Getting There' (*CP*, pp. 247–9), Plath uses death not to symbolise actual physical death but regeneration, in keeping with the Tarot card associated with death, the Reaper. '. . . what is depicted here is the death of the old self, the sloughing off of all fleshly desires.' (Frank Lind, *How to Understand the Tarot*, 1979, p. 43.)

19 Ibid, pp. 41–42.

20 Plath kept her own hive of bees while living in Devon.

21 The hermit in this poem is partly inspired by the Tarot card 'the Hermit', who is depicted as a seeker of mystical wisdom.

22 Here the influence of Dylan Thomas is very apparent (as for example in 'The Force that through the Green Fuse drives the Flower', *Selected Poems, 1934–1952*, 1986, p. 8.)

23 The repetition of symbols parallels the repetition of key words from poem to poem. From the beginning of her adult career, in 1956, when Plath worked assiduously with a thesaurus beside her, to the free-floating verse of her last published poems some words are carried from poem to poem. This repetition of words and images creates a strong leitmotif in her work and provides further evidence for seeing her work as an organic whole. In a Lecture for the British

Academy at The British Academy in Oxford 1981 the linguist C S Butler carried out a computer analysis of Plath's stylistic development, highlighting changes in word frequency, range of vocabulary, word and sentence length together with other semantic features. His examination of Plath's system of colours shows that 'while the distribution of most of the frequent colour-terms is similar in the four volumes of poems, [referring to *The Colossus*, *Crossing the Water*, *Ariel* and *Winter Trees*, the last three published in edited editions by Ted Hughes] their collocational behaviour (that is, the kinds of lexeme with which they tend to associate) may vary with the stages in the poet's development.' (C S Butler 'Poetry and the Computer: Some Quantative Aspects of the Style of Sylvia Plath', *Proceedings of the British Academy*, Vol. 15, 1979.)

24 *LH*, p. 342.

25 Plath's use of smiles contradicts neatly the image put forward by the all-pervasive advertising industry in the USA at that time, which sold every product to the public with a smile. A note in her *Journals* from 1958 shows how she saw this as the badge of conventionality: 'Smile, write in secret, showing no one.' (*Journals*, p. 259.)

26 The necessity for women to take control of their lives was a concern taken up by feminist poets, prominent among them Plath's rival and respected fellow-poet Adrienne Rich.

27 This echoes a passage in *The Bell Jar*, in which the heroine Esther voices her discontent with the conventional stance adopted by her boyfriend and his mother in their attempts to make her conform: 'He was always saying how his mother said, "What a man wants is a mate and what a woman wants is infinite security," and, "What a man is is an arrow into the future and what a woman is is the place the arrow shoots off from," until it made me tired.' (*The Bell Jar*, p. 74.)

28 Plath had voraciously devoured J G Fraser's *The Golden Bough* and Robert Grave' *The White Goddess*,

so she was again in this instance defying traditional conceptions and in her own way creating a new tradition.

29 This 'ecological' viewpoint of Plath's, held decades before it was fashionable to be 'green' is given a negative though realistic outcome in the poems 'Totem' (*CP*, pp. 264–45) and 'Contusion' (*CP*, p. 271).

30 Much of her work was inspired by art; Giorgio de Chirico is the influence behind 'The Disquieting Muses' (*CP*, pp. 74–6) and 'Conversation Among the Ruins' (*CP*, p. 21) (*Journals*, p. 210); in an interview Plath said 'a lot of my poems take off from visual images', (Sylvia Plath *The Poet Speaks*) Paul Klee is behind 'The Ghost's Leavetaking' (*CP*, pp. 90–1); while Rousseau has influenced 'Yadwigha, on a Red Couch, Among Lilies' (*CP*, pp. 85–6).

31 In a talk by A Alvarez, 'The Poetry of Sylvia Plath' (BBC Third Programme, 23 September 1963) he commented on how a major feature of her method was to let image breed image and that this was ruled by an 'intelligent control of her feelings'.

32 Sylvia Plath, Broadcast, 'Contemporary Poetry' BBC Third Programme, 10 January, 1963.

33 Siegfried Krakauer, *Theory of Film*, 1978, p. 39.

34 Ingmar Bergman, in much of whose work the past becomes part of the present (Ibid p. 235) is a strong influence on much of Plath's later work. The verse play 'Three Women' (*CP*, pp. 176–87) was inspired directly by him. (*LH*, p. 456.) In this connection it is interesting to note Plath's annotation to her copy of Eliot's *Four Quartets*: 'We live by memory of the past (the dead) and we are born again by memory of events in the past . . . time is not unredeemable – past can exist in present; present can always be a fresh beginning.' (Sylvia Plath, copy of *Four Quartets*, now in possession of the Rare Book Room, Neilson Library, Smith College.)

35 'When I'm describing Henry James' use of metaphor to make emotional states vivid and concrete, I'm dying to be making up my own metaphors. When I hear a

professor saying: "Yes, the wood is shady, but it's a *green* shade – connotations of sickness, death, etc.", I feel like throwing up my books and writing my own bad poems and bad stories and living outside the neat, gray secondary air of the university. I don't like talking *about* D H Lawrence and about critics' views of him.' (*LH*, p. 330.)

36 Plath's use of metaphor was an assertive progression from her remarkable use of other figurative language, such as similes, for example, in 'Insomniac' (*CP*, p. 163): '. . . invisible cats/Have been howling like women, or damaged instruments.'

37 *LH*, p. 343.

38 R Phillips, *The Confessional Poets*, 1973, p. 9.

39 Sylvia Plath, op. cit.

40 Ibid.

41 'I like Joyce Cary – I have that fresh, brazen, colloquial voice. Or J D Salinger. But that needs an "I" speaker, which is so limiting.' (Sylvia Plath, *Journals*, p. 156.)

Chapter 8.

1 Alicia Ostriker, *Stealing the Language*, 1987, p. 60. It is significant that Plath's BA thesis was on the double in Dostoevsky's novels.

2 *Journals*, pp. 42–3.

3 *LH*, p. 333.

4 *LH*, p. 34.

5 *LH*, p. 34.

6 *LH*, pp. 34–5.

7 *LH*, p. 68.

8 *LH*, p. 35. Plath's commercial prose writing was a double-edged sword. As Ted Hughes has commented, part of the problem with her prose initially stemmed from the fact that 'she was always trying to write a pastiche of the sort of writing she imagined was wanted by the journal she had in mind'. (Introduction to *JP*.) In *The Bell Jar*, however, Plath overcame this ambivalence.

9 One night she reported to her mother about a triple

date she had been on: 'Rod asked me what grade I got. I said airily, "All A's, of course." "Yeah," he replied, grinning, as he led me out to the dance floor. "You *look* like a greasy grind!" Oh, Mummy, they didn't believe me; they didn't believe me!' (*LH*, p. 38.)

10 *LH*, p. 45.

11 *LH*, p. 234. And she saw herself doing this in a full and positive way: 'I shall be one of the few women poets in the world who is fully a rejoicing woman'. (*LH*, p. 256.)

12 Alicia Ostriker, op. cit., p. 60.

13 *LH*, p. 297.

14 *LH*, p. 329.

15 *Journals*, p. 272.

16 *LH*, p. 343.

17 Robert Lowell, Foreword to the American edition of Sylvia Plath's *Ariel*, 1966, p. ix. Plath at this point was apparently like the female speaker/protagonist in 'Tulips' (*CP*, pp. 161–2) '. . . I have no face, I have wanted to efface myself.'

18 A Alvarez recalled how he had first met her. Calling by the Hughes' small flat in Primrose Hill to pick up Ted for a walk and interview in Regent's Park, Alvarez had been thanked by Plath for publishing one of her poems and she had to remind him who she was: 'For Christ's sake, Sylvia *Plath*! It was my turn to gush, "I'm sorry. It was a lovely poem". . . . I was embarrassed not to have known who she was. She seemed embarrassed to have reminded me, and also depressed.' A Alvarez, *The Savage God*, 1972, pp. 23 and 25.

19 The journal extracts, not intended for publication, give a different if fragmented view of her as a writer. She emerges from the insecure and introspective young woman of 1956, whose notes read almost like diary entries, into the detached artist of 1962, who has the aesthetic detachment required to be able to draw on her own experience as material for her work. Much of the observation recorded in these entries provided the basis for her poetry and prose.

20 *LH*, p. 466. Plath knew that they were of a high enough quality to make up a volume of poetry.

21 *LH*, p. 468.

22 One of Plath's fears as a young woman was to be regarded as an arid, asexual being like so many of the academics around her, whom she both admired and despised. *LH*, p. 198 *et passim*.

23 Apparently the woman lying next to Plath when she was in hospital was 'wrapped almost completely in a plaster cast'. (E Butscher, *Sylvia Plath: Method and Madness*, 1976, p. 267.)

24 The poems are a part of the writer which are immortal.

25 This is a poem which expresses its vision in a comic Gothic tone with images and situations reminiscent of Charles Addams' sketches.

26 Here Plath echoes the same predicament felt by countless women writers.

27 *Journals*, p. 210. Several of Plath's poems were influenced by artists and sculptors, such as Jackson Pollack, Klee, Breughel and Baskin. Ingrid Melander has researched the influence of art on Plath's work in her dissertation 'The Poetry of Sylvia Plath: A Study of Themes', University of Gothenburg, 1971.

28 In a radio broadcast of this poem Plath introduced it as follows: 'It borrows its title from the painting by Giorgio di Chirico – The Disquieting Muses. All through the poem I have in mind the enigmatic figures in the painting – three terrible, fearless dressmaker dummies in classical gowns, seated and standing in a weird, clear light that casts the long shadows characteristic of di Chirico's early work. The dummies suggest a twentieth-century version of other sinister trios of women – the Three Fates, the witches in Macbeth, de Quincey's sisters of madness'. (Note, *CP*, p. 276). Plath had referred to herself as a 'triple-threat woman'. (Sylvia Plath quoted in Lois Ames, 'Notes towards a Biography' in *New Views on the Poetry*, edited by Gary Lane, 1979, p. 166).

29 Ellen Moers, in her excellent study *Literary Women*

(1978) has outlined the special power the Gothic gave to Plath: 'It was Plath herself, with her superb eye for the imagery of self-hatred, who renewed for poets – Anne Sexton, Adrienne Rich, Erica Jong, and many others – the grotesque traditions of Female Gothic.' (pp. 109–10.)

30 In its anarchic and gothic humour, this poem is distinctly reminiscent of the work of Stevie Smith.

31 Appropriately, she named her second book of poetry after a poem which celebrates rebirth, particularly the redemptive nature of art. The 'eye' is a pun on I and the drive which links the various levels of this poem occurs in the process of lovemaking and riding a horse bareback over the moors, and this fusion succeeds through an emphasis on 'the cauldron' which is synonymous with the melting-pot of art.

32 My italics.

33 Ted Hughes' note to this poem reads 'Bronze dead men lay in numbers around the house and studio.' Note, *CP*, p. 287.

34 A more romanticised view of the recluse than that shown in 'Two Sisters of Persephone'.

35 Echoes of Dylan Thomas are very much apparent here.

36 At this point of her life Plath was 'getting up at five in the morning to write down poems in blood'. (Sylvia Plath quoted in Elizabeth Sigmund, 'Sylvia in Devon: 1962, 1967, p. 105.)

37 The search for identity was also the distinguishing feature of American writers and artists in the 1950s: 'Where the search for community had captured the imagination of the Left in the 1930s, the search for identity inspired the writers and artists of the 1950s.' Richard Pells, quoted in William O'Neill, *The Years of Confidence* 1945–1960, 1986, p. 24.

38 Suzanne Juhasz, *Naked and Fiery Forms: Modern American Poetry by Women: A New Tradition*, 1976, p. 4.

39 *LH*, p. 403.

40 *LH*, p. 475.

41 Alicia Ostriker, 'Fact as Style: The Americanization of Sylvia', in *Language and Style*, No. 1, Summer 1968, p. 205.

42 In a letter to her mother in 1957 Plath had pointed out her dissatisfaction with contemporary English poetry: 'It is often infuriating to read the trash published by the Old Guard, the flat, clever, colorless poets here (in America there is, with much bad, still much color, life and vigor).' *LH*, p. 293. A Alvarez commented on Plath's approval of his introduction to *The New Poetry*, which had been published the previous spring (London, 1962): 'In it I had attacked the British poets' nervous preference for gentility above all else, and their avoidance of the uncomfortable, destructive truths both of the inner life and of the present time. Apparently, this essay said something she wanted to hear; she spoke of it often and with approval, and was disappointed not to have been included among the poets in the book.' (A Alvarez *The Savage God*, op. cit., p. 40.)

43 The influence of the Confessional poets on her work is much in evidence in a number of Plath's later poems, such as 'Poem for a Birthday' (1959, *CP*, pp. 131–8), a poem inspired by Roethke and also by the classic German film Metropolis, and 'Lesbos' (*CP*, pp. 227–30), which deals with a relationship between two women. Plath commented on the Confessional poets who had particularly influenced her at that time: 'I've been very excited by what I feel is the new breakthrough that came with, say, Robert Lowell's *Life Studies*, this intense breakthrough into very serious, very personal, emotional experience which I feel has been partly taboo. Robert Lowell's poems about his experience in a mental hospital, for example, interest me very much. These peculiar, private and taboo subjects, I feel, have been explored in recent American poetry. I think particularly the poetess Anne Sexton, who writes about her experience as a mother, as a mother who has had a nervous breakdown, is an extremely emotional and feeling young woman and her poems

are wonderfully craftsman-like poems and yet they have a kind of emotional and psychological depth which I think is something perhaps quite new, quite exciting.' Sylvia Plath, quoted in *The Poet Speaks: Interviews with Contemporary Poets*, edited by Peter Orr, 1966, pp. 167–8. And in her radio broadcast 'New Comment: Contemporary American Poetry', BBC Third Programme 10 January 1963, Plath pointed out the omission from *The New Poetry* collection of Anne Sexton's work: 'The poems in her remarkable second book *All My Pretty Ones* could stand up to the best of anything here.'

44 Sylvia Plath *The Poet Speaks*, op. cit., pp. 169–70.

45 'Plath associates sexual and medical violence, links the personal and the institutional, the private and the public in a way that has become one of the hallmarks of the feminist analysis of power.' (Jacqueline Rose, *The Haunting of Sylvia Plath*, p. 123.)

46 Robin Morgan commented that much criticism of Plath's work has been a 'conspiracy to mourn [her] brilliance while patronizing her madness, diluting her rage,/burying her politics.' ('Arraignment', in *Monster*, 1972, p. 78.)

47 'Context', in *JP*, p. 98.

48 Ibid.

49 There are poems Plath wrote which are still missing. In a letter to George Macbeth, dated 4 April 1962 (now in possession of the BBC Written Archives at Caversham) Plath sent 'a batch of recently unpublished poems for your perusal . . . I particularly enjoy "Afterlife". "Mother Superior" and "Ash" make my hair stand on end: I think they are fine.' (Letter from Sylvia Plath to George Macbeth.) It is not known what has happened to these poems.

50 'The Bell Jar', directed Larry Pearce, 1978, starring Marilyn Hackett, a melodramatic piece which was withdrawn shortly after it was first performed. 'Sylvia Plath', choreographed by Johann Kresnik and performed by the Heidelberg Stadtheater in 1987 was a powerful piece of theatre, which, through

extensive use of her work, made a creditable attempt to represent her.

51 'Sylvia Plath Reading Her Poetry', in *Great American Poets*, (cassette), Caedmon, 1987. In the first ten months of publication *Ariel* sold over 5000 copies and *The Bell Jar* over 50,000 a year.

52 'Context', *JP*, p. 99.

53 A Alvarez, op. cit., p. 55.

Chapter 9.

1 Plath was encouraged to take ballet and piano lessons, her ineptitude for which she aptly satirises in the poem 'The Disquieting Muses' (*CP*, pp. 74–6).

2 Linda Wagner-Martin, *Sylvia Plath – A Biography*, 1988, p. 44.

3 'Bitter Strawberries' (*CP*, pp. 299–300) was based on Plath's experience in a summer job at a nearby farm; the poem made the appropriate connection between the transience of youth to the waste of life in the Korean War.

4 Linda Wagner-Martin, op. cit., p. 44. Much later in her life, when her dreams of an ideal marriage were shattered, Plath showed her generosity of spirit; in a letter to her brother and sister-in-law she wrote: 'The one thing I retain is love for and admiration of [Ted's] writing. I know he is a genius and for a genius there are no bonds and no bounds.' *LH*, p. 467. One of her Smith roomates, Nancy Hunter Steiner recalled how Plath took pleasure in making her birthday a special day: 'I was Alice, Boston was Wonderland, and Sylvia had prescribed it for me in 'small, mirthful doses'. *A Closer Look at Ariel*, 1974, p. 26.

5 Plath had already unsuccessfully submitted work no less than 45 times to *Seventeen* when an editor told her to read every issue she could lay her hands on to pick up the house style. (*LH*, p. 35.)

6 Linda Wagner-Martin, op. cit., p. 45.

7 The US population was expanding at a rate comparable to India. The values of America seemed at

that time to be 'those of the middle class suburb moulded by the demands of mass production and the mass media of communication'. (D K Adams, *America in the Twentieth Century* 1967); *America and the Americans*, edited by Edmund Fawcett and Tony Thomas, 1983, pp. 96–7.

8 *LH*, p. 72.

9 *LH*, p. 40.

10 *LH*, p. 3. It was to Olive Prouty that Plath intended to dedicate the American edition of Ariel. (*LH*, p. 478.)

11 *LH*, p. 83.

12 *Method and Madness*, p. 69.

13 Adlai Stevenson told the Smith graduates that their role in life was to give purpose and wholeness to their men. This assignment was to be of great benefit to them: 'In the first place, it is home work – you can do it in the living room with a baby in your lap, or in the kitchen with a can opener in your hands. If you're really clever maybe you can even practise your saving arts on that unsuspecting man while he's watching television.' Adlai Stevenson, quoted in *Another Part of the Fifties*, Carter, 1983, p. 87.

14 *LH*, p. 85.

15 Wendy Campbell, 'Remembering Sylvia', in *The Art of Sylvia Plath*, edited by Charles Newman, 1970, p. 18.

16 Linda Wagner-Martin, op. cit., p. 98.

17 Ibid, p. 97.

18 In November 1962 a letter from Plath prompted Dr Beuscher to ask her to come to the States and stay with her, but she was reassured by a subsequent letter which indicated that Plath was managing to cope after all. Linda Wagner-Martin, op. cit., p. 230.

19 Ibid p. 109. With her suicide, Plath was in a sense capitulating to what the feminist psychologist Phyllis Chesler termed one of the 'grand rites of "feminity" – i.e. ideally, women were supposed to "lose" in order to "win." Women who *succeed* at suicide are, tragically, outwitting or rejecting their "feminine" role, and at

the only price possible: their death.' (*Women and Madness*, 1972, p. 49.)

20 *A Closer Look at Ariel*, p. 54. A passage from *The Bell Jar*, in which Plath compares the inmates of a psychiatric hospital to college girls in the 1950s makes it clear how aware Plath was of the dangers of conformity: 'What is there about us in Belsize, so different from the girls playing bridge and gossiping and studying in the college to which I would return? These girls, too, sat under bell jars of a sort.' (*BJ*, p. 251) In fact, the bell jar of the fifties! An article she wrote for *Punch* magazine, 'America! America' (*JP*, pp. 40–4) focused on the all-pervasive pressure to conform.

21 *LH*, p. 228.

22 Linda Wagner-Martin, op. cit., p. 126.

23 *Journals*, p. 113. (Note that the omissions are the editor's, not mine.)

24 *Journals*, p. 153. Marriage also offered Plath a chance to escape her mother's influence. Plath and her mother were very close, but, as with every mother-daughter relationship, this closeness was sometimes constricting. As Aurelia commented: 'Between Sylvia and me there existed – as between my own mother and me – a sort of psychic osmosis which, at times, was very wonderful and comforting; at other times an unwelcome invasion of privacy.' (*LH*, p. 32.)

25 *Journals*, p. 146.

26 *LH*, p. 240.

27 Linda Wagner-Martin, op. cit., p. 110.

28 *Journals*, p. 293.

29 *Journals*, p. 259. As a writer, she saw her rivals as 'in history Sappho, Elizabeth Barrett Browning, Christina Rossetti, Amy Lowell, Emily Dickinson, Edna St Vincent Millay – all dead . . . Now: Edith Sitwell and Marianne Moore, the aging giantesses, and poet godmother Phyllis McGinley is out – light verse: she's sold herself. Rather: May Swenson, Isabella Gardner, and most close, Adrienne Cecile Rich.' (*Journals*, p. 211.)

30 *Journals*, p. 196.
31 *Journals*, p. 211.
32 Linda Wagner-Martin, op. cit., p. 159.
33 *Anne Sexton and Her Critics*, edited by J D McClatchy, 1978, p. 168.
34 *LH*, pp. 201–2.
35 Ibid, p. 205.
36 Aurelia Schober Plath, 'Sylvia Plath's Letters Home – some reflections by her mother', *The Listener*, 22 April 1976, p. 516.
37 One of the many letters to her mother on the subject shows how important it was for Plath that her husband be successful before her: 'I am so happy *his* book is accepted *first*. It will make it so much easier for me when mine is accepted – if not by the Yale Series, then by some other place. I can rejoice then, much more, knowing Ted is ahead of me.' (*LH*, p. 297.)
38 Later she was to write one of her own in 1959, *The Bed Book*, published in 1976, light and humorous, and still selling well.
39 Linda Wagner-Martin, op. cit., p. 214.
40 Ibid, p. 215.
41 *LH*, p. 468.
42 *Me Again: Uncollected Writings of Stevie Smith*, edited by Jack Barbera and William McBrien, 1981, p. 6. They never met as Plath died less than three months later.
43 *LH*, p. 475.
44 R Hayman, *The Death and Life of Sylvia Plath*, 1991, p. 179.
45 *LH*, p. 469.

Selected Bibliography

Works by Sylvia Plath
(abbreviations as used in text)

Plath, S, *Ariel*, Faber and Faber, London, 1965; Harper and Row, New York, 1966.

—*The Bed Book*, Faber and Faber, London, 1976.

—*The Bell Jar* [BJ] Heinemann, London, 1963; Faber and Faber, 1966; Harper and Row, New York, 1971.

—Cambridge Manuscript, English Faculty Library Cambridge, 1957. [submitted by Sylvia Plath towards part 2 of her Tripos.]

—*The Collected Poems* [CP], edited by Ted Hughes, Faber and Faber, London, 1981.

—*The Colossus and Other Poems*, Heinemann, London, 1960; Alfred Knopf, New York, 1962.

—*Crossing the Water*, Faber and Faber, London, 1971; Harper and Row, New York, 1972.

—*Crystal Gazer*, Rainbow Press, London, 1971.

—*The Journals of Sylvia Plath* [Journals], edited by Ted Hughes and Frances McCullough, The Dial Press, New York, 1982.

—*Johnny Panic and the Bible of Dreams* [JP], Faber and Faber, London, 1977; second edition with additional stories from the Sylvia Plath collection at the Lilly Library, 1990.

—*Letters Home* [LH], edited by Aurelia Plath, Faber and Faber, London, 1975; Harper and Row, New York, 1975.

—*Lyonesse*, Rainbow Press, London, 1971.

—'The Magic Mirror: A Study of the Double in Two of Dostoevsky's Novels', Undergraduate honours thesis, Smith College, 1955.

—*Uncollected Poems*, Turret Press, London, 1965.

—*Winter Trees*, Faber and Faber, London, 1971; Harper and Row, New York, 1972.

—*Wreath for a Bridal*, Sceptre Press, Frensham, 1970.

—Unpublished material from the Sylvia Plath Collection,

Rare Book Room, Smith College Library, North-ampton, Mass., USA

Studies related to Sylvia Plath mentioned in the text

Books

Aird, E, *Sylvia Plath*, Harper and Row, New York, 1973.

Alvarez, A, *The Savage God*, Weidenfeld and Nicholson, London, 1971; Random House, New York, 1972.

Butscher, E, *Sylvia Plath: Method and Madness*, Seabury Press, New York, 1976.

Gubar, S, and Gilbert, S M, *The Madwoman in the Attic*, Yale University Press, New Haven and London, 1979.

Hayman, R, *The Death and Life of Sylvia Plath*, Heinemann, London, 1991.

Hedberg, J, *Poets of Our Time: English Poetry from Yeats to Sylvia Plath*, Stockholm, 1970.

Holbrook, D. *Sylvia Plath: Poetry and Existence*, Athlone Press, London, 1976.

Juhasz, S, *Naked and Fiery Forms: Modern American Poetry by Women: A New Tradition*, Harper Colophon, New York, 1976.

Moers, E, *Literary Women*, The Women's Press, London, 1978.

Newman, C, (ed.) *The Art of Sylvia Plath: A Symposium*, Faber and Faber, London, 1970.

Orr, P, (ed.) *The Poet Speaks: Interviews with Contemporary Poets*, Routledge & Kegan Paul, London, 1966.

Ostriker, A, *Stealing the Language*, The Women's Press, London, 1987.

Rose, J, *The Haunting of Sylvia Plath*, Virago, London, 1991.

Salop, L, *Suisong*, Vantage Press, New York, 1978.
Steiner, N H, *A Closer Look at Ariel: A Memory of Sylvia Plath*, Faber and Faber, London, 1974.

Wagner-Martin, L, *Sylvia Plath: A Biography*, Simon and Schuster, New York, 1987; Chatto and Windus, London, 1988.

Articles

Ames, L, 'Notes towards a Biography', *New Views on The Poetry*, edited by Gary Lane, The Johns Hopkins Press, Baltimore and London, 1979.

Bernikow, L (ed.) *The World Split Open: Four Centuries of Women Poets in England and America, 1551–1950*, The Women's Press, London, 1979.

Butler, C S, *Poetry and the Computer: Some Quantitative Aspects of the Style of Sylvia Plath*, Chatterton Lecture on an English Poet, British Academy, Vol. LXV, Oxford University Press, London, 1979.

Campbell, W, 'Remembering Sylvia' *The Art of Sylvia Plath*, edited by Charles Newman, Indiana University Press, Bloomington, 1970.

Chesler, P, *Women and Madness*, Avon, New York, 1972.

Ferrier, C, 'The Beekeeper's Apprentice', *New Views on the Poetry*, edited by Gary Lane, The Johns Hopkins Press, Baltimore and London, 1979.

Hardy, B, 'The Poetry of Sylvia Plath', *Women Reading Women's Writing*, edited by Sue Roe, Harvester Press, Brighton, 1987.

Hughes, T, 'Ariel', *The Poetry Book Society* Bulletin, No. 44, February 1965.

Hughes, T, 'Notes on the Chronological Order of Sylvia Plath's Poems', *The Art of Sylvia Plath*, edited by Charles Newman, Indiana University Press, Bloomington and London, 1970.

Lavers, A, 'The World as Icon – on Sylvia Plath's Themes', *The Art of Sylvia Plath*, edited by Charles Newman, Indiana University Press, Bloomington and London, 1970.

MacQuarrie, J, *An Existential Theology*, Penguin, Harmondsworth, 1980.
—*Existentialism*, Penguin, Harmondsworth, 1987.
McClatchy, J D, 'Short Circuits and Folding Mirrors', *Sylvia Plath: New Views on the Poetry*, edited by Gary Lane, John Hopkins Press, Baltimore, 1979.
Martin, W, 'God's Lioness – Sylvia Plath: Her Prose and Poetry', *Women's Studies*, Vol. 1., 1971.
Melander, I, 'The Poetry of Sylvia Plath: A Study of Themes', University of Gothenburg, Diss, 1971.

Newlin, M, 'The Suicide Bandwagon', *Critical Quarterly*, No., 14, 1972.

Oakley, A, *Subject Women*, Collins, London, 1981.
Oates, J C, 'The death throes of romanticism', *Southern Review*, No. 9, 1973.
Ostriker, A, 'Fact as Style: The Americanization of Sylvia', *Language and Style*, Vol. 1, Summer 1968.

Perloff, M, 'Angst and Animism in the Poetry of Sylvia Plath', *Journal of Modern Literature*, No. I, 1970.
Phillips, R, *The Confessional Poets*, Southern Illinois University Press, Carbondale and Edwardsville, 1973.
Plath, A S, 'Sylvia Plath's Letters Home – some reflections by her mother', *The Listener*, 22 April, 1976.

Rich, A, 'Conditions for Work', *On Lies, Secrets and Silence – Selected Prose 1966–1978*, Virago, London, 1980.
—'When We Dead Awaken: Writing as Re-Vision', *On Lies, Secrets and Silence*, Virago, London, 1980.
Rosenthal, M L, 'Sylvia Plath and Confessional Poetry', *The Art of Sylvia Plath*, edited by Charles Newman, Indiana University Press, Bloomington, 1970.

Scarborough, M N, 'Songs of Eleusis: The Quest for Self

in the Poetry of Sylvia Plath, Anne Sexton and Adrienne Rich,' University of Michigan, 1978.

Schmidt, M and Lindop, G. (ed.) *British Poetry since 1960*, Carcanet, Oxford, 1972.

Sigmund, E, 'Sylvia in Devon: 1962', *Sylvia Plath: The Woman and the Work*, edited by Edward Butscher, Dodd, Mead & Co, New York, 1977.

Sumner, N McCowan, 'Sylvia Plath', *Research Studies*, No. XXXVIII, June, 1970.

Thwaite, A 'Out of the Quarrel: On Sylvia Plath', *Encounter*, No. LIII, 1979.

Uroff, M D, 'Sylvia Plath on Motherhood'. *The Midwest Quarterly*, Vol. 25, No. 1, 1973.

van Dyne, S, 'More terrible than she ever was: The Manuscripts of Sylvia Plath's Bee Poems', Smith College Library Rare Book Room, 1982.

Vendler, H, 'An Intractable Metal', *The New Yorker*, 15 February, 1982.

Watts, Emily Stipes, *The Poetry of American Women from 1632 to 1945*, University of Texas Press, Austin, 1977.

Other relevant studies

Adams, D, K, *America in the Twentieth Century*, Cambridge, 1967.

Alexander, P (ed.) *Ariel Ascending: Writings about Sylvia Plath*, Harper & Row, New York, 1985.

—*Rough Magic*, Viking, Penguin, New York, 1992.

Alvarez, A (ed) *New Poetry*, Penguin, Harmondsworth, 1962.

—'Poetry in Extremis', *London Observer*, 14 March, 1965.

Anna, P J, *A disturbance in mirrors*, Greenwood Press, New York, 1988.

Annas, Pamela J, 'The Self in the World: The Social Content of Sylvia Plath's Late Poems', *Women's Studies*, Vol. 7, Nos. 1/2, 1980.

Axelrod, S G, 'Plath's and Lowell's Last Words', *Pacific Coast Philology*, No. 11, 1976.
—*Sylvia Plath: the wound and the cure of words*, Johns Hopkins University Press, 1990

Barnard, C, K, *Sylvia Plath*, Twayne Publishers, Boston, 1978.
Bassnett, S, *Sylvia Plath*, Macmillan, London, 1987.
Berbera, J and McBrien, W (eds) *Me Again: Uncollected Writings of Stevie Smith*, Farrar, Straus, Giroux, New York, 1981.
Bennet, P, *Emily Dickinson: Woman Poet*, Harvester Wheatsheaf, Hemel Hempstead, 1990.
Birstein, A, 'The Sylvia Plath Cult', *Vogue*, 158, 1 October, 1971.
Boyers, P, 'Sylvia Plath: The Trepanned Veteran', *The Centennial Review*, Vol. 131, No. 2, 1969.
Broe, M L, 'Recovering the Complex Self: Sylvia Plath's Beeline', *The Centennial Review*, Vol. 24, No. 1, 1980.
—*Protean Poetic. The Poetry of Sylvia Plath*, University of Missouri Press, Columbia and London, 1980.
Brownjohn, A, 'A Way Out of the Mind', *The Times Literary Supplement*, 12 February, 1982.
Bundtzen, L K, *Plath's Incarnations: Woman and the Creative Process*, The University of Michigan Press, Ann Arbor, 1983.
Byatt, A S, 'Mirror, Mirror on the Wall', *New Statesman*, 23, April 1976.

Camus, A, *L'étranger*, Gallimard, Paris, 1957.
Carter, P A, *Another Part of the Fifties*, Columbia University Press, New York, 1983.
Cox, C B and Jones, A R, 'After the Tranquillized Fifties', *Critical Quarterly*, No. 9, 1964.

Davison, P, *Half Remembered: A Personal History*, Harper & Row, New York, 1973.
Dickie, M 'The Alien in Contemporary American Women's Poetry', *Contemporary Literature*, 23 March, 1987.
Donovan, Josephine, 'Sexual Politics in Sylvia Plath's Short Stories', *The Minnesota Review*, No. 4, 1973.

Eisenstein, H, *Contemporary Feminist Thought*, Unwin, London, 1984.

Farnham, M and Lundberg, F, *Modern woman – the lost sex*, 1947.

Fawcett, E and Thomas, T (eds) *America and the Americans*, Collins, London, 1983.

Ferguson, M A, *Images of Women in Literature*, Houghton Mifflin, Boston, 1973.

Fraser, G S, 'A Hard Nut To Crack From Sylvia Plath', *Contemporary Poetry*, No. 1, 1973.

Fraser, J G, *The Golden Bough*, London, 1890.

Freud, S, *An outline of psychoanalysis*, The Hogarth Press, London, 1969.

Friedan, B, *The Feminine Mystique*, Norton, New York, 1963.

Gordon, Jan B, 'Who is Sylvia? The Art of Sylvia Plath', *Modern Poetry Studies*, No. 1, 1970.

Graves, R *The White Goddess*, Farrar, Straus, Giroux, New York, 1948.

Hamburger, M, *The Truth of Poetry: Tension in Modern Poetry from Baudelaire to the 1960s*, Weidenfeld and Nicolson, London, 1969.

Hardwick, E, 'On Sylvia Plath', *New York Review of Books*, No. VII, 12 August, 1971.

Hoffman, N J, 'Reading Women's Poetry: The Meaning and Our Lives', *College English*, Vol. 34, No. 1, 1972.

Howe, I, 'Sylvia Plath: a partial disagreement', *Harper's Magazine*, No. 244, January, 1972.

Hughes, T, 'Sylvia Plath and Her Journals', *Grand Street*, Vol. 1, No. 3, 1985.

Jones, A R, 'Necessity and Freedom: The Poetry of Robert Lowell, Sylvia Plath and Anne Sexton', *Critical Quarterly*, No. 7, 1965.

King, P R, *Nine Contemporary Poets*, Methuen, London, 1979.

Kinsey, A, *Sexual Behavior in the Human Male*, W B Saunders, London, 1948.

—*Sexual Behaviour in the Human Female*, W B Saunders, London, 1953.

Krakauer, S, *Theory of Film*, Oxford University Press, Oxford, 1978.

Kroll, J, *Chapters in a Mythology: The Poetry of Sylvia Plath*, Harper & Row, New York, 1976.

Kyle, B, *Sylvia Plath: A Dramatic Portrait*, Harper & Row, New York, 1977.

Lawrence, D H, *Apocalypse*, Viking Compass, 1931.

—*Fantasia of the Unconscious and Psychonalysis and the Unconscious*, Penguin, Harmondsworth, 1977.

—*The Collected Short Stories*, Heinemann, London, 1974.

—*Women in Love*, Harmondsworth, Penguin, 1960.

Lehrer, S, *The Dialectics of Art and Life: A Portrait of Sylvia Plath as Woman and Poet*, Universitat Salzburg, Institut fur Anglistik und Amerikanistik, 1985.

Libby, A, 'God's Lioness and the Priest of Sycorax: Plath and Hughes', *Contemporary Literature*, Vol. 15, No. 3, 1974.

Lind, F, *How to Understand the Tarot*, Aquarian Press, Wellingborough, Northants. 1979.

McClatchy, J D (ed.) *Anne Sexton and Her Critics*, Indiana University Press, Bloomington and London, 1978.

McLuhan, M, *The Medium is the Massage*, Bantam, New York, 1967.

Macpherson, P, *The Puzzle of Sylvia Plath*, University of Kent, Canterbury, 1983.

Malkoff, K, *Escape from the Self: A Study in Contemporary American Poets and Poetics*, Columbia University Press, New York, 1977.

Marzack, R, *Sylvia Plath*, The Open University Press, 1992.

Matovich, R M, *A Concordance to the collected poems of Sylvia Plath*, Garland, New York and London, 1986.

Meakin, D, *Man & Work*, Methuen, London, 1976.

Meissner, W, 'The Rise of the Angel: Life Through Death in the Poetry of Sylvia Plath', *Massachusetts Studies in English*, Vol. 3, No. 2, 1971.

Middlebrook, Wood D, and Yakom, M (eds) *Coming to Light: American Women Poets in the Twentieth Century*, University of Michigan Press, Ann Arbor, 1985.

Mizejewski, L, 'Sappho to Sexton: Woman Uncontained', *College English*, No. 35, December 1973.

Mollinger, F N, 'A Symbolic Complex: Images of Death and Daddy in the Poetry of Sylvia Plath', *Descant*, Vol. 19, No. 2, Winter, 1975.

Morgan, R, *Monster*, Random House, New York, 1972.

Murdoch, B, 'Transformations of the Holocaust: Auschwitz in Modern Lyric Poetry', *Comparative Literature Studies*, Vol. 11, No. 2, June, 1974.

Nguyen, Than-Binh, 'A Stylistic Analysis of Sylvia Plath's Semantics', *Language and Style*, Vol. 11, No. 2, 1978.

Novak, Robert, *Sleeping with Sylvia Plath*, Windless, Orchard, 1983.

O'Neil, W, *The Years of Confidence; 1945–1960*, The Free Press, New York, 1986.

Oberg, A, *Modern American Lyric: Lowell, Berryman, Creeley, and Plath*, Rutgers University Press, New Brunswick, NJ, 1978.

Owen, W, 'A Riddle in Nine Syllables: Female Creativity in the Poetry of Sylvia Plath', *DAI*, Vol. 47, No. 4, 1986.

Perloff, Marjorie, 'Extremist Poetry: Some Versions of the Sylvia Plath Myth', *Journal of Modern Literature*, Vol. 2, No. 4, 1972.

Propociov, N, 'Sylvia Plath and the New England Mind', *Thoth*, Vol. 13, No. 3, Fall, 1973.

Rich, A, *Snapshots of a Daughter-in-Law*, Chatto & Windus, London, 1970.

Riesman, D, *The Lonely Crowd: A Study of the Changing American Character*, Yale University Press, New Haven and London, 1950.

Rosenblatt, J, 'Sylvia Plath: The Drama of Initiation', *Twentieth Century Literature*, Vol. 25, No. 1, 1979.

—*Sylvia Plath: The Poetry of Initiation*, University of North Carolina Press, Chapel Hill, 1979.

212

Rosenstein, H, 'Reconsidering Sylvia Plath', *MS Magazine*, 1 September 1972.

Rosenthal, M L, *The New Poets: American and British Poetry Since World War II*, Oxford University Press, New York, 1967.

Salinger, J D, *Catcher in the Rye*, Penguin, Harmondsworth, 1951.

Sartre, J P, *Being and Nothingness*, Methuen, London, 1981.

Scheerer, C, 'The Deathly Paradise of Sylvia Plath', *The Antioch Review*, Vol. 34, No. 4, 1976.

Schwartz, M and Bollas, C F, 'The Absence at the Center: Sylvia Plath and Suicide', *Criticism*, Vol. 18, No. 2, 1976.

Shakespeare, W, *The Tempest*, in *The Complete Works of Shakespeare*, Collins, Glasgow, 1951.

Simpson, L, *A Revolution in Taste: Studies of Dylan Thomas, Allen Ginsberg, Sylvia Plath and Robert Lowell*, Macmillan, New York, 1978.

Smith, P A, 'The Unitive Urge in the Poetry of Sylvia Plath', *New England Quarterly*, Vol. 45, No. 3, 1972.

Snively, S R, 'The Language of Necessity: The Poetry of Sylvia Plath', Boston University Graduate School, Boston, 1976.

Srivastava, A K, 'The Intense Flame: Letters and Poems of Sylvia Plath', *Indian Journal of American Studies*, Vol. 11, No. 1, 1981.

Stevenson, A, *Bitter Fame*, Penguin, London, 1989.

Thomas, D, *Selected Poems*, Dent, London, 1986.

Tillich, P, *The Courage to Be*, Yale University Press, New Haven, 1952.

Thomas, Professor T, *Sylvia Plath: Last Encounters*, Bedford, 1989.

Uroff, M D, *Sylvia Plath and Ted Hughes*, University of Illinois Press, Urbana, Chicago and London, 1979.

—'Sylvia Plath's Women', *Concerning Poetry*. Vol. 7, No. 1.

Vendler, H, *Part of Nature, Part of Us. Modern American Poets*, Harvard University Press, Cambridge, 1981.

Wagner, L (ed.) *Critical Essays on Sylvia Plath*, G K Hall, Boston, 1984.

Wagner, L W, 'Plath's The Bell Jar as Female Bildungsroman', *Women's Studies*, Vol. 12, No. 1, 1986.

Walsh, T P and Northouse, C, *Sylvia Plath and Anne Sexton: A Reference Guide*, G K Hall, Boston, 1974.

Woolf, V *To the Lighthouse*, Penguin, Harmondsworth, 1988.

—*Three Guineas*, Penguin, Harmondsworth, 1977.

Index of Poems

Aftermath, 91, 112–113
Alicante Lullaby, 71
All the Dead Dears, 83, 184, 188
Among the Narcissi, 83, 106, 124
Appearance, An, 85
Applicant, The, 66–7, 85, 92, 131
Apprehensions, 64–5, 118, 120
Ariel, 8, 28–30, 121, 122–3, 124,
   129–30, 141, 172, 173, 175, 184
Arrival of the Bee Box, The, 11, 36,
   116–17

Babysitters, The, 27
Barren Woman, 141
Beekeeper's Daughter, The, 116, 168
Bee Meeting, The, 11, 116, 119, 122
Berck-Plage, 46, 57, 61–2, 120, 121,
   126–7, 172, 175, 189
Birthday Present, A, 40, 81, 103
Bitter Strawberries, 200
Black Rook in Rainy Weather,
   139–40
Blue Moles, 101–2
Brasilia, 55–6, 120, 173
Bull of Bendylaw, The, 114–15
By Candlelight, 32–3

Child, 33–4
Colossus, The, 112
Contusion, 104, 193
Conversation Among the Ruins,
   111, 193
Couriers, The, 80–1, 141, 172, 184
Crystal Gazer, 115
Cut, 78, 91–2, 128

Daddy, 9, 15–16, 58, 75, 77, 79–80,
   82, 95, 96, 118, 123, 128
Death & Co., 46–8, 82, 122, 172
Detective, The, 122
Dialogue Over a Ouija Board,
   115, 180
Disquieting Muses, The, 30, 31, 83,
   140–1, 193, 200

Eavesdropper, 24–5, 28, 172
Edge, 2, 35, 48–9, 77, 114, 122, 123,
   125, 176

Electra on the Azalea Path, 112
Elm, 25–6, 28, 128
Everlasting Monday, The, 115
Eye-Mote, The, 112

Face Lift, 36–7, 72, 81
Faun, 112
Fever 103°, 17, 40, 41–2, 75, 85,
   97–8, 103, 122, 178
Finisterre, 59–60
Full Fathom Five, 57

Getting There, 14, 38–40, 66, 95–6,
   99, 122, 124, 167, 191
Ghost's Leavetaking, The, 71, 80,
   184, 188, 193
Gigolo, 11, 73
Goring, The, 187
Green Rock, Winthrop Bay, 101

Hanging Man, The, 115, 116
Heavy Women, 71
Hermit at Outermost House, The,
   120, 142–3

I am Vertical, 43–4
In Midas Country, 112
In Plaster, 139
Insomniac, 90, 126, 194
I Want, I Want, 58

Jailer, 14

Kindness, 80, 124, 143, 175–6

Lady and the Earthenware Head,
   The, 83
Lady Lazarus, 16–17, 37–8, 56,
   81–2, 84–5, 91, 94–5, 96, 120, 122,
   131–2, 164, 191
Last Words, 43, 44
Leaving Early, 19–22, 23, 28, 81
Lesbos, 21–4, 28, 75, 81, 123,
   170, 198
Letter in November, 66, 78, 107,
   120, 125
Little Fugue, 118
Lorelei, 115
Lyonesse, 56, 77, 115

Magi, 61, 76–7, 119
Mary's Song, 33, 60, 61, 103
Medallion, 102
Medusa, 30, 31, 59, 113–14
Metaphors, 32, 72–3, 128
Mirror, 123
Moon and the Yew Tree, The, 62–4, 119, 123, 141, 174, 179
Moonrise, 118
Morning Song, 11, 32, 35
Munich Mannequins, The, 175
Mushrooms, 118–19
Mystic, 17-18, 67–8, 125, 129

Nick and the Candlestick, 33, 77–8
Night Shift, 89, 124
November Graveyard, 105

Ode for Ted, 10
On Deck, 61, 80
Other, The, 122

Paralytic, 40–1
Perseus, 112
Pheasant, 12, 102
Poem for a Birthday, 83, 198
Point Shirley, 118
Poppies in July, 124, 129, 173
Poppies in October, 106–7, 120, 124, 125, 129
Private Ground, 62, 102
Purdah, 13–14, 82, 113, 129

Rabbit Catcher, The, 12
Recantation, 115, 118
Rival, The, 27

Sculptor, 142–3
Sheep in Fog, 124, 164, 174, 179
Sleep in the Mojave Desert, 104–5
Snakecharmer, The, 120, 142
Sonnet: To Eva, 130
Sow, 73–4
Spider, 114

Spinster, 13, 76
Stillborn, 190
Stings, 11, 99, 117, 119
Strumpet Song, 12
Swarm, The, 11, 74, 99, 117, 122

Thalidomide, 103
Thin People, The, 188
Three Women, 11, 31–2, 49, 54–5, 60, 107–8, 119, 120, 125, 167
Times are Tidy, The, 79
To Eva Descending the Stair, 130
Totem, 49–50, 56–7, 90, 114, 119, 124, 129, 180, 193
Tour, The, 80, 83–4, 93–4, 99, 141, 184, 187
Tulips, 40, 42–3, 107, 124, 129, 195
Two Campers in Cloud Country, 105–6, 173
Two Sisters of Persephone, 112, 138–9
Two Views of a Cadaver Room, 10, 44–5, 76

Virgin in a Tree, 74–5, 112

Watercolour of Grantchester Meadows, 104
Whiteness I Remember, 118
Whitsun, 81, 90
Widow, 14
Wintering, 11, 19, 35, 79, 117, 169
Winter Landscape, with Rooks, 111–12
Winter Trees, 26–7
Words, 2, 4, 35, 49, 143, 165
Wuthering Heights, 105

Yadwigha, On a Red Couch, Among Lilies, 130, 193
Years, 49, 65
You're, 128

Zoo Keeper's Wife, 12, 27